Soap Opera Babylon

Soap Opera Babylon

JASON BONDEROFF

A PERIGEE BOOK

Perigee Books
are published by
The Putnam Publishing Group
200 Madison Avenue
New York, NY 10016

Photo credits: pages 10, 16 (left), 22, 29, 30, 33, 37, 95,
128, CBS; pages 16 (right), 26, 40, 41, 59, 65, 80, 81,
87, 101, 111, 117, 120, 131, 134, 141, ABC; pages 38,
50, 55, 56, 75, 105, 107, 124, 138, NBC; page 13, Universal Pictures; page 37, Avco Embassy; page 90, Gold
Coast Film Corp.; pages 34, 48, 58, 129, author's collection. Photos on pages 36, 43, 69, 84, 93, 123, 125, cour-
tesy of Allen Rosenberg, Sterling's Magazines Inc.

Library of Congress Cataloging-in-Publication Data

Bonderoff, Jason.
Soap opera babylon.

1. Soap operas—United States. 2. Television
actors and actresses—United States—Biography.
I. Title.
PN1992.8.S4B66 1987   791.45′75′0973   86-30294
ISBN 0-399-51291-8

Book design by The Sarabande Press

Printed in the United States of America

1 2 3 4 5 6 7 8 9 10

CONTENTS

9   The Kiss of Death?

19   Drugs and Alcohol

32   Backstage Bitchery and Blind Ambition

46   Blood Money

62   And Baby Makes Three

72   Death Wish

79   The Casualties of *General Hospital*

94   Backstage Affairs

109 The *Dynasty* Dolls

122 Baring Their All and Other Skeletons in the Closet

132 Backstage at the Soaps

140 S.O.B. Awards

Soap Opera Babylon

THE KISS
OF
DEATH?

The set is hushed. The red light outside the studio door goes on. Even the cameramen are tense. Ashley Abbott and her wealthy married lover, Victor Newman, are about to climb into bed together for the first time. It's a scene that devout *Young and Restless* fans have been anticipating for months.

As the actors slowly disrobe, an electrifying stillness ignites the air. Victor smiles; Ashley sighs. And the seduction begins. Ah yes, this is what soap opera is all about—ravished hearts and rumpled beds. And nobody does it better than the nubile stars of *The Young and the Restless*.

Victor sweeps Ashley up in his arms and carries her off to bed. But then—just when their lips are barely a millimeter apart—the camera suddenly pulls back.

What's going on here? Where's the torrid, tantalizing payoff we expected? There must be some mistake. Isn't this the same show where David Hasselhoff and Lynn Topping, as Snapper and Chris, once spent so much time in bed that the producer offered to bring a nurse on the set to rotate them? Didn't redhead Jaime Lyn Bauer—who played the raunchy Lori Brooks Prentiss—soul-kiss one leading man so hard that he was practically begging for mercy? (Or was he begging for more?)

Whatever happened to those sultry moments? Has Hollywood put them in permanent cold storage?

For the time being at least, it looks like romance-at-room-temperature is here to stay. Why? Fear of sexually transmitted diseases—particularly, AIDS. Shows like *The Young and the Restless, Dallas,* and *Dynasty*—in fact, all the soaps—are keeping steamy love scenes down to a minimum. Long, hot contact between actors is no longer being encouraged.

Owing to the current AIDS epidemic in Hollywood—and the fear that's running rampant along with it—nobody wants to get too close for comfort. Starlets and studs circle each other warily on the set now. The days of diving down each other's throat are out. One actress with a lot of contract clout on *All My Children* demanded proof—in the form of a blood test—that her leading man had nothing to hide. He refused to take the test. She got a new leading man.

Married and macho Eric Braeden's love scenes with Eileen Davidson were toned down on The Young and the Restless.

Even straight actors are feeling the heat—or rather a distinct lack of it. As Hunt Block, who plays Peter Hollister on *Knots Landing,* jokes, "Let's put it this way—when Donna Mills and I kiss, there's a lot less exchanging of bodily fluids now!"—but the joke has a hollow ring to it. Too many actresses are running scared. In fact, Eileen Davidson—the stunning young beauty who plays Ashley Abbott on *The Young and the Restless*—flatly refuses to take any unnecessary risks on the air. She won't do more than lightly brush lips with any of her handsome costars, even if they bring in notes from their mothers (and girlfriends) certifying how straight they are. So what if Eric Braeden, who plays her bed companion, Victor Newman, is both macho and married in real life? The show purposely toned down their most intimate love scenes because Eileen didn't want to appear to be playing favorites. How could she agree to do an open-mouthed kissing scene with one actor and not another? She might as well be pointing an accusing finger and saying, "I find your sexuality very suspicious." Instead Eileen just decided to keep her "mouth shut" with all her leading men, period.

Eileen's off-screen fiancé, actor Chip Mayer, jokes that he's found the perfect way to protect her on the set. "I simply paint sores on her neck and lesions on her mouth before she goes to work," he says. "That way she never has to worry about any leading man wanting to get too close to her!" He also advises her to eat onion sandwiches and garlic pickles before a big love scene—a technique that's guaranteed to keep any costar at arm's length. In fact, if Eileen's lucky, it might even knock the poor guy out for the rest of the show.

But ultimately it's no laughing matter. Eileen and dozens of other soap opera sirens are facing an anguished choice. What's worse? Possibly exposing yourself to AIDS infection—or risking unpopularity on the set?

There's been so much backstage hysteria on *The Young and the Restless* that the producers brought in a medical expert to try to calm the cast. "We talked to the doctor and he said, 'Oh, there's no danger with kissing—it's perfectly safe,' " Eileen recalls, "but what does that mean? One actress on the show asked him, 'If your wife was on a soap opera, would you want her to kiss a stranger?' Well, the doctor paled. He squirmed in his seat and finally, very quietly, said no. Not very reassuring, is it? So now the producers have made it an individual thing. It's up to each of us to decide how far we'll go on the air.

"In a way, I think it's harder for soap actresses than anybody else in this business. Let's say Meryl Streep makes a film. Who does she work with? Robert Redford or Dustin Hoffman. Does she really have to worry about catching anything? They shoot the kissing scenes a few times, and then it's over. But when you're working on a soap, they're bringing in new actors every day and you're frequently doing love scenes with total strangers. You never know who's going to try to get his personal kicks by forcing his tongue down your throat—and you don't know where he's been the night before, do you?"

The furor began innocently enough with Rock Hudson—the quintessential Hollywood he-man—kissing Linda Evans on *Dynasty*. It turned out to be the last love scene he would ever film. Just a few months after completing his *Dynasty* commitment, the fifty-nine-year-old actor shattered all our boy-next-door illusions forever and publicly admitted he had AIDS. By the time Rock died in his Beverly Hills home on October 2, 1985, the possible consequences of that fateful on-screen encounter had become a matter of national debate. Had Rock risked Linda's life by exposing her to the deadly virus, too? Should gay actors be banned from doing love scenes—or at least forced to take a medical test for AIDS before being cast in heavily romantic roles? Hollywood was shaking right down to the seat of its Guess jeans. At the same time that Rock Hudson lay dying, the Screen Actors Guild issued a policy statement declaring open-mouthed kissing as "possibly hazardous work."

The fact that Rock Hudson was gay surprised almost no one. Despite his virile heterosexual screen image, Rock's insatiable man-chasing had been known to the Hollywood community for years. One of Rock's companions, Jim Gagner, told biographer Sara Davidson: "His sexual energy was so extreme, you could feel the heat. It made my ears burn. He could have sex once or twice a day with several different people."

Rock's life-style was certainly his own business—and homosexuals are hardly a downtrodden minority in the acting world. But his decision to accept a guest-starring role on *Dynasty*—and to kiss Linda Evans—was something else again. He already knew he was dying when *Dynasty* coproducer Esther Shapiro approached him about taking on the role of millionaire-adventurer Daniel Reece, a character slated to become romantically involved with Linda Evans (Krystle Carrington).

In June of 1984 Rock had been diagnosed as suffering from Kaposi's sarcoma, a rare form of cancer directly attributable to AIDS. Two months later he went to Paris, where he was treated with experimental drugs; and after that his condition seemed to improve for a short time. In October he began working on *Dynasty,* but he couldn't entirely disguise his rapidly failing health. It was hard to believe that the gaunt, thin, ravaged-looking star who showed up on the set was the same Rock Hudson who had once

In 1965, when Hudson wooed Gina Lollobrigida in Strange Bedfellows, *actresses were thrilled to do intimate love scenes with him.*

dominated the screen with his charismatic presence in films like *Giant* and *Magnificent Obsession*. Hudson wandered around the *Dynasty* set like a ghost. He was constantly fatigued. He had no appetite. He spent all his free time sleeping in his dressing trailer. Worst of all, he frequently had trouble memorizing his lines.

The cast and crew began to suspect he was ill, but figured he was probably just trying to shake off a virus. Jack Freeman, the show's makeup man, told *TV Guide,* "His coloring was very pale. I did what I could to make him look better, but I think it was evident that he wasn't really well or strong." When the script called for Daniel Reece to survive a plane crash, Hudson had to film the scene outdoors on a brutally cold morning. He was shivering from head to toe, but couldn't wear a heavy coat because it would destroy the reality of the scene. Costar John Forsythe noticed how ill Hudson looked and offered to bring him a cup of tea or coffee. Hudson refused. He was determined to keep playing "the rugged, indomitable hero," no matter what. His worst fear—possibly worse than facing the physical ravages of AIDS itself—was that people might find out. True, he would later change his mind on that subject and become the first Hollywood star to make a public declaration that he was suffering from what has now been called the black plague of the 20th century. But at that point Hudson wasn't ready for martyrdom. He was still desperately trying to hold on to his image, his star stature, his career. It was all he had left.

Maybe that's why he forced himself to go through with that kissing scene on *Dynasty*. He simply couldn't bear the humiliation of confronting Esther Shapiro, admitting that he had AIDS, and then facing dismissal from the show. He found out about the kiss a week before he had to shoot it. He discussed it with friends, agonized over it, and finally decided to say nothing. On the day of the shooting he was extremely distraught, but still in enough control to orchestrate the scene exactly the way he wanted it. He gargled repeatedly with mouthwash and used antiseptic mouth spray before going on the set. During the actual filming, he kissed Linda Evans with his lips closed, barely touching her on the mouth. That way there was very little chance of any saliva being exchanged. In a macabre way, Hudson's years of experience as a great screen lover paid off: by kissing her on the cheek, very close to her mouth (which the camera only caught from one side), he was able to make the kiss look far more intense than it really was. To Linda Evans his behavior must have seemed almost prudish, but she kept her thoughts to herself. Knowing that Hudson was gay, she probably attributed his standoffishness to the fact that he really didn't care to touch women.

Less than six months after his final *Dynasty* episode aired, Rock Hudson was dead. The news must have been especially chilling to Linda Evans, but outwardly she remained calm and unruffled. "His death is a great loss to all of us, but his legacy will be our continued fight for a cure for AIDS," she said. And even perfect-lady Krystle Carrington couldn't have phrased it better when Linda told reporters, "I haven't had blood tests and I haven't been concerned about my health at any point." But insiders on the *Dynasty* set suspected otherwise. If Linda had known in advance about Hudson's illness, would she still have agreed to work with him? A lot of people thought not.

The entire incident left lots of questions unanswered. After all, how could the show's producers have hired Hudson in such far from robust condition? Didn't they have any inkling at all how sick he was? Maybe not. Somehow Hudson—a master actor right up to the end—had managed to fool everyone, even his live-in lover, Marc Christian. Up until the summer of 1985, Marc thought Rock was merely suffering from anorexia, not anything communicable, as he watched him slowly waste away. "I found out he had AIDS on the six o'clock news like everyone else."

The obituary list is rapidly growing. During the last few years, actors on four daytime soaps—*Guiding Light, Another World, Santa Barbara,* and *Edge of Night*—have all died of the disease, and recently Paul Keenan, a Hollywood actor barely turned thirty, was hospitalized with AIDS. In 1982 he played Todd Chandler on *Days of Our Lives*.

In New York and L.A. the good times still roll, but there's a new sense of caution. At setside parties, the champagne flows, just as it always did, but nobody's drinking out of anybody else's cup anymore. Under the klieg lights the mood is even bleaker. Former *Knots Landing* star Lisa Hartman admits she'd be "worried" if she had to face something like the Linda Evans/Rock Hudson situation. Donna Mills, the show's resident sex kitten, is even more vocal on the subject: "AIDS has spread so much that I don't want to kiss anyone new on the show," she announced recently.

Okay, Sharon Gless and Tyne Daly don't have to worry much. On crime shows like *Cagney & Lacey,* characters are more likely to get mugged than hugged, but on prime-time soaps making out is a way of life. Silver-haired veterans like *Falcon Crest*'s Jane Wyman may get to handpick their leading men, but most actresses have to rely on the luck of the draw—and it's a risky business even with a leading man who's straight as an arrow.

"Sometimes you want to carry your own supply of penicillin with you," says Linda Gibboney, an actress who's worked on *All My Children, Search for Tomorrow,* and *Santa Barbara.* "There's a story going around the studios about an actress who was doing a love scene and she said to her leading man, 'What's that on your lip?' He said, 'Oh, just a cold sore'—and now she has herpes." Another herpes sufferer—a hot-blooded daytime

Left: *"I always feel safe kissing Mark Lewis," says* Guiding Light's *Krista Tesreau. "After all, I even know his girlfriend."* Right: General Hospital's *Tony Geary and Genie Francis, undoubtedly the most romantic couple ever on daytime TV, did more than just pay lip service to the script.*

heartthrob—was able to keep doing love scenes by carefully covering up the telltale signs with makeup. His totally trusting young costar never knew. A while later, when she realized she'd contracted the disease, her boyfriend threw her out (they'd been living together for three years) because he was sure she'd cheated on him.

But it's not easy to say no on the set—especially if you're young and inexperienced and hungry for work. "I've been on shows where I've worried that I might catch something from the guy I had to kiss," admits one starlet who'd rather not be mentioned by name, "but it's so hard to get jobs in this town, who wants to blow a guest spot on prime time because somebody's lip looks funny? He might have been in a fight last night for all I know. The one thing you don't need is a reputation that you're hard to work with—a prima donna, if you know what I mean."

Devon Ericson had a hot kissing scene on *Airwolf,* but it didn't faze her in the least. "That guest stint was good prime-time exposure," she says. "When I came home from work that day and told a friend of mine about the scene, she was hysterical. She said, 'How could you do it? You don't even know this guy or where he's been!' But I can't think that way—or work that way. If I did, I might as well quit acting and become a nun. Besides," she laughs, "the only thing I ever caught from one of my costars was a head cold!'"

But more and more the consensus of opinion is: better safe than sorry. Most actresses have stopped borrowing each other's lipstick and mascara. On the *Dallas* set, Priscilla Presley, Linda Gray, and Victoria Principal have their own makeup kits, and other stars are following suit. In the wake of the AIDS crisis, it's getting increasingly expensive to stock the studio makeup rooms, since throwaway cosmetics are now the rule, not the exception. Actors are refusing to use products that have touched the lips and faces of other actors.

According to *TV Guide,* many stars are seeking legal advice. Beverly Hills attorney Marvin Mitchelson was consulted by an actress who wanted to know if she could refuse to do a love scene with a leading man who was notoriously bisexual. She asked if she could insist that the actor take a blood test before she agreed to work with him. "I told her I thought she could," says Mitchelson. "After all, it is a reasonable kind of fear to be afraid for your life."

When actress Sharon Gabet was playing Raven Whitney on *The Edge of Night,* one of her costars continued working on the show after he was stricken with AIDS. At the time, Sharon was pregnant and petrified that the virus might somehow be transmitted to her baby. She later gave birth to a healthy little girl, but the memory of those tense months still haunts her. "I'll never forget how that man looked and acted," she says. "He was very sickly and had terrible coughing fits on the set all the time. We didn't have any love scenes together, but I felt very uncomfortable and scared just being around him all day. It was an awful situation."

Why did *Edge of Night* continue to employ an actor who was so visibly ill? For one thing, as long as an actor shows up for work, ready and willing to do his job, it's difficult to let him go. For another, there's no scientific proof that casual contact spreads AIDS. And ultimately the bottom line is this: most producers don't have the time or inclination to deal head-on with the issue. Not with ratings to watch, union crews to contend with, contracts to negotiate, and a thousand and one other hassles. Besides, what recourse does an actress have if her producer happens to be gay himself?

There are no easy answers. "I'm not terrified about getting the disease," says Linda Dano, who plays Felicia Gallant on *Another World.* "I don't think you get it just by casual kissing. But I think there's an even bigger consideration here—loyalty. Some of my dearest friends are in the gay community. How can I march into a producer's office and say, 'I won't do a scene with that person because he's gay!' If a situation like that ever arose, I'd sit down—one on one—and talk it over with the actor. I hope we could discuss openly, and without embarrassment, what we'd each feel comfortable doing in the scene. And we'd work it out ourselves. The important thing is, no matter what, I wouldn't turn my back on him."

DRUGS
AND
ALCOHOL

*T*he drug culture is everywhere in show business, and even the soaps aren't immune. Ivory Snow may be 99 and 44 one-hundredths-percent pure, but it's a very different kind of snow that circulates among the actors in some quarters.

An actor on a New York soap was hooked so heavily on cocaine that the show eventually had to give him a leave of absence to straighten himself out. He spent a few weeks in a private rehabilitation center, then returned to work, determined not to fall into the same trap again. A few days after he was back at the studio, a friend of his showed up in the lobby, demanding to see him. The actor refused to come out of his dressing room, but he begged the studio guard not to call the police and have the uninvited guest arrested. The "friend" in question was his former cocaine dealer. The last thing in the world he wanted to do was get the police involved. After a few days the dealer stopped hanging around the studio, but the actor was so afraid of running into him that he still came and went through a freight entrance at the back of the studio. Neighborhood fans, who liked to hang out at the front entrance of the studio, assumed this formerly approachable star was suddenly pulling a Sean Penn. Little did they know what he was really running from.

∎ ∎ ∎

A few years back the stars of a top-rated daytime soap spent an afternoon sailing on a rented boat while they filmed an extravagant yacht-party scene. The boat was anchored several miles from shore—far, far away from the everyday confines of the studio—and the real partying that went on was a lot wilder than anything in the script.

The shoot dragged on for hours and hours, much longer than anyone had expected. Bad weather was partially responsible for the delay, but that wasn't the primary reason for all the holdups. According to one witness, there was so much cocaine being passed around that some actors had no idea if it was foggy or not. As the day wore on, one actress became violently ill. Between the constant rocking of the boat and all the cocaine in her system, she kept throwing up and delaying production even more. Even when she wasn't being sick, she kept forgetting her lines and missing her mark. Considering how high she was, it's amazing she didn't fall overboard and drown.

■　　■　　■

The rugged young hero of another soap was turned into a pill-dependent loser for reasons viewers never suspected. The actor who played the role was hooked on amphetamines in real life—and his drug dependency was interfering with his work. He was too valuable to lose, but impossible to work with. When he was down, he couldn't remember his lines, he'd forget to show up for rehearsal, and he'd practically bump into the furniture on the set. When he was up, he'd invent whole new sections of dialogue right on the air, leaving the actors who had to respond to him lost and panic-stricken. He was so scattered that he had no idea why the rest of the cast was lined up against him. In his distorted way of thinking, the producer was simply out to get him, and the other actors were all jealous of his enormous popularity.

If he hadn't been such a fan favorite, the producer probably would have thrown him off the show. But the network considered him indispensable, so the top brass came up with a rather unique solution: they'd simply let him play himself. On the air his character became an overnight speed freak and suddenly the actor's erratic behavior was an on-screen asset, not a liability. In the end it all worked out rather well. Over a period of months, as the storyline progressed, the actor managed to kick his own habit (in part because so much pressure was taken off him at work)—and the story of his character's downfall and subsequent recovery proved to be a huge ratings-grabber.

■　　■　　■

Some stars clean up their act before landing on soaps. Jess Walton, who plays Kelly Harper on *Capitol,* had a drug problem during her early Hollywood days (when she was romantically involved with the manager of a top rock-'n'-roll band). It was a time when she was living on the fringes of the limelight. "I was very vulnerable," she admits. "I used drugs and drank to protect myself. When I was thirty-three, I stopped. I replaced it with spiritual values. I'd had enough. My life was going nowhere. It embarrasses me now to think I acted stoned."

In the last few years she's turned her life around completely, thanks to her marriage to a grief counselor named John James (no relation to the *Dynasty* star) and the birth of their son Cole, now five.

•   •   •

Patrick Francis Bishop—a young Asian-American heartthrob—went through hell several times during his days as a struggling entertainer. Before he won the role of Yank, a dedicated medical resident on *General Hospital,* Patrick was a drifter in the music world. His vagabond life-style—touring India, Thailand, and Australia with a rock band—led to life-threatening bouts of hepatitis and tuberculosis. Along the way there were on-and-off battles with drugs, too, dating all the way back to his teenage years. Finally, though, he came to the realization that instead of giving him an identity, drugs were just helping him to throw his life away. Now even marijuana doesn't tempt him. "In Hollywood everything is wide open, but it's not for me anymore," he says. "I've been down that road and still have the scars within to prove it." He's now a nonsmoker, nondrinker, and confirmed vegetarian. "I've given up just about every vice except women," he laughs.

•   •   •

Falcon Crest's Lorenzo Lamas also once used drugs. Lamas is a man full of complex passions. Sometimes it's hard to distinguish the real Lorenzo from Lance Cumson, the spoiled-brat playboy he portrays on CBS every Friday night. They're both drawn like magnets to fast cars and fast women—and give the impression that they're nursing some kind of uncontrollable death wish.

In November 1985 Lorenzo nearly died when his car bashed into a concrete wall during a 110-mile-an-hour run at Riverside International Raceway in California. At first eyewitnesses thought he was dead. It took

Lorenzo Lamas grew up on the wild side—and still moves to a fast and furious beat.

paramedics almost half an hour to pull him out of the wreckage and, believing he had a broken neck, they immediately encased him in a neck brace. Fortunately his injuries were less serious—just a broken collarbone and a dislocated shoulder. According to Jim Hyneman, the raceway's public relations director, "Lorenzo had God on his side—he was the luckiest man in the world to come out of this alive."

The producers of *Falcon Crest* were furious. They ordered Lorenzo to stay off the auto track, but he laughed in their faces. "I'm not giving up," he said defiantly. "I just got tired and lost my concentration for a minute when I hit the wall, but I love racing too much to walk away from it."

It wasn't his first high-speed crackup. In the spring of 1985 he nearly signed his death warrant during a practice run at Willow Springs, California. He was racing on the same track with *Riptide*'s Perry King. They were neck and neck when King's engine suddenly blew up and his car went hurtling off the track. Within seconds Lorenzo lost control of his own vehicle. It flipped in the air, made a 360-degree circle, landed on its wheels, and slammed into a retaining wall. "When I got out of the car, it was totaled. Broken in half," Lorenzo recalls. He walked away from that mishap with barely a scratch. But eight years before he hadn't been so lucky. A fall off a motorcycle left him with a cracked skull that required thirty-six stitches. He was partially paralyzed and unable to speak for three days. But it didn't diminish his taste for daredevil antics.

He's been making headlines (and headaches) practically since the day he walked on the *Falcon Crest* set. His first marriage—to a woman twelve years his senior—barely lasted a year. He divorced her to marry his second wife, who was already pregnant with his child. When that marriage hit the skids, he developed a $500-a-week cocaine habit.

Falcon Crest costar Abby Dalton calls Lorenzo a little boy locked in an adult body. "Lorenzo's vision of reality is like some kind of fairy tale, and he has to learn otherwise if he ever expects to grow up," she warns.

But then again he's been living a fairy tale all his life. Back in the 1950s, both his parents were bonafide Hollywood royalty. His mother, Arlene Dahl, was Rita Hayworth's successor as queen of the screen vamps; his father, Fernando Lamas, was the renowned Latin lover. Obviously it made for a fiery—but hardly substantial—mix. They were divorced by the time Lorenzo was two. Shortly afterward his father married Esther Williams, while Arlene embarked on an endless matrimonial merry-go-round (at last count she was either wedding or shedding husband number six).

After the divorce Lorenzo spent his early years with his mother in New York, but he was mainly raised by a succession of nannies and housekeepers. When Arlene entertained, Lorenzo served a homemade wine-and-vodka concoction to glitterati like Van Johnson and Norma Shearer. They thought his antics were cute, but despite his outward sophistication, Lorenzo remained a lonely, troubled kid. He worshiped his father, whom he rarely saw. He was overweight and felt ugly. "I was an emotionally troubled child," Lorenzo later said. "I ate a lot out of frustration to compensate for the kind of deprivations I had." (Interestingly enough, as a teenager Lorenzo turned to bodybuilding and, as an added macho touch, he had three tattoos emblazoned on his arm and shoulder.)

During his adolescence Lorenzo began to spend more time with his father and stepmother in California. He'd already been kicked out of several prestigious boarding schools. (His favorite prank was putting fireworks in teachers' desk drawers.) He also got his first taste of moviemaking when he accompanied his father on location in Spain. The elder Lamas was costarring with Burt Reynolds and Raquel Welch in *100 Rifles,* and Lorenzo had a bit part as an Indian boy.

After graduating from a stiff military academy in New Jersey and then marking time at the University of California at Santa Barbara, Lorenzo landed a small part in the movie *Grease.* Next came two TV series that didn't make it—*California Fever* and *The Secrets of Midland Heights*—and then his big break on *Falcon Crest.*

Falcon Crest debuted in 1981. The following year his father died and Lorenzo went into an emotional tailspin. He'd married model Victoria Hilbert (who was thirty-five to his twenty-three) against his father's strenuous objections. Now, ten months after the wedding ceremony, he walked out on her to marry twenty-five-year-old publicist Michele Smith, whom he'd met at New York's Studio 54. Lorenzo filed for divorce in September 1982; he was hoping to wait a little longer before marrying Michele, but her pregnancy intervened. Their quickie wedding took place aboard a yacht in Marina Del Ray on May 22, 1983. At the time Lorenzo crowed: "I can see myself living with this girl forever. She's so easy and makes no demands. We just support each other's lives."

Not long afterward their son Alvaro Joshua (nicknamed A.J.) was born. But—despite Lorenzo's contention that this union was a rhapsody of love—things went sour very quickly. By the fall of 1984 the marriage was in serious trouble, and both Lorenzo and Michele were heavily into cocaine. "We certainly hit rock bottom," Lorenzo told journalist Sharon Rosenthal. "I was going through a thousand dollars every two weeks. I was high most of the time." Despite his cocaine habit, Lorenzo still managed to get up at six every morning and report to work. But he was existing in a hazy, horrifying limbo. He was doing coke first thing in the morning and last thing at night—not just at parties anymore, but in his own house, a sure sign of deepening dependency. It had become "a very scary drug," Lorenzo remembers, "because the only person you're partying with is yourself."

He quit "cold turkey" in January 1985 and soon afterward instituted divorce proceedings against Michele, who, he claimed, was still hooked. He also sued for custody of A.J., alleging that Michele's drug habit was so bad that her negligence was tantamount to child abuse. The child's nanny, Mrs. Mendoza, corroborated Lorenzo's charges. She publicly stated that Michele was partying almost every night behind locked doors in her bedroom and had occasionally passed out. Even Michele's own mother, Mrs. Joy Smith, told the court: "I have known about Michele's illness and instability for some time." In May 1985 the court granted temporary custody to Michele, but stipulated that the child's nanny must always be present. (Later, though, Michele and Lorenzo seemed to be coming to terms and were actually working out plans to share the upbringing of the boy.)

Meanwhile, Lorenzo's list of romantic liaisons continues—including Jennifer O'Neill, Ana Alicia, *Too Close for Comfort* star Lydia Cornell, and Abby Dalton's daughter, Kathleen Kinmont Smith (whom he dated both before and after his marriage to Michele). Like so many Hollywood stars, he can't seem to get off the roller coaster. He lives for the next surge, the next wave, the next intoxicating breakaway.

■   ■   ■

James Farentino—the actor who played diabolical Dr. Nick Toscanni on *Dynasty*—has made his share of stupid and dangerous mistakes, too. At one point his drinking and his "bad attitude on the set," as producers put it, kept him from getting work in Hollywood. It also cost him his marriage to *Knots Landing* star Michele Lee. But a young actress named Deborah Mullowney (who now plays Sloane Denning on *Capitol*) helped him exorcise his demons and turn his life completely around.

Deborah was only twenty-one when she fell hot and heavy for Farentino, and nothing could keep her away from him. She wasn't scared off by his reputation as a Hollywood hell-raiser, his two failed marriages, or the fact that he was more than twenty years her senior—old enough, in fact, to be her father.

Farentino was virile and handsome. Deborah was a stunning, delicate-featured brunette. But the attraction was more than just physical. From the moment they struck up their first conversation (in a Los Angeles acting class), Deborah was literally mesmerized by the man—flattered perhaps that a star of Farentino's magnitude was bothering to pay any attention to her. After all, Deborah was just a novice on the acting scene, fresh out of San Jose State, where she'd majored in biology and theater arts. So far her résumé was pretty thin. Her only professional credits were a few modeling jobs in New York and Paris.

Farentino, of course, was a familiar screen personality—maybe not a megastar, but still a name to be reckoned with. In 1963 (when Deborah was learning to pedal her first tricycle) Farentino was already making his movie debut in *The War Lord* with Charlton Heston. By the time Deborah reached junior high school, Farentino had done two TV series of his own—*The Bold Ones* and *Cool Million*—and was now back in New York head-lining at Lincoln Center in an acclaimed revival of *A Streetcar Named Desire*. The *New York Times* theater critic wrote that Jimmy Farentino was better than Brando as Stanley Kowalski. But somehow none of it added up to superstardom. Despite everything he had going for him—talent, opportunity, good looks—Farentino couldn't make the jump from nice-enough-leading-man-with-second-billing up to the realm of the Redfords and Pacinos where he really belonged.

By the time Deborah Mullowney came into his life, James Farentino was in his mid-forties. Turning-point time. But whatever disappointments and regrets were locked inside him, on the surface he seemed secure and confident, possibly the most engaging man Deborah had ever met. In fact, he was a refreshing change for her. In college, she'd dated jocks and business-school types; afterward, in Los Angeles, she'd encountered a lot of would-be young actors who bored her. They tended bar or waited tables somewhere, and spent more time looking for the "right" acting

On Dynasty *John Forsythe and James Farentino were mortal enemies.*

teacher than they did looking for work. None of them were ready for a real relationship. Farentino was. With his charm and vitality, he soon overshadowed them all.

In 1982 things started heating up between them. At that time Farentino was working on *Dynasty*—playing Dr. Nick Toscanni—a sexy (and psychopathic) psychiatrist whose libido was always operating on fast forward. Nick hopped into the sack with Fallon (Pamela Sue Martin) and came close to seducing her stepmother Krystle (Linda Evans), too. But if Deborah worried about Jimmy's steamy love scenes with *Dynasty*'s breathtaking beauties, she never let on. After all, she knew he hadn't exactly lived a cloistered life before meeting her.

Far from it. At times his own life had seen enough passion—and fireworks—to make a rip-roaring soap opera. First there was his infamous marriage to Elizabeth Ashley—their relationship was a disaster from start to finish. In 1963, after a year of marriage, they split (she took up with George Peppard) and Farentino soon became involved with another actress, Michele Lee. (She later told *People* magazine, "I offered him a shoulder to cry on. He did—then he cried on other parts of my body.") In 1966 Farentino and Michele were married in a civil ceremony (a neat solution since the bride was Jewish and the groom was Catholic). But later on Michele insisted that their son, David, attend Hebrew school and be raised as a Jew.

Their erratic fifteen-year marriage was a kind of emotional endurance test. The scenario included battles, breakups, reconciliations, marriage counseling, and a final split in 1981 that left them both winded—and wounded.

Like most show-business divorces, the state of their respective careers added fuel to the fire. All through the 1960s and 70s, Michele's success had been minor compared to her husband's, but in 1979 her role on the new prime-time soap *Knots Landing* catapulted her to prominence. As Karen Fairgate, she soon emerged as one of television's most popular heroines. Farentino joined *Dynasty* in 1981, but his character, Dr. Nick Toscanni, was a doomed villain—a charming but expendable foil who made John Forsythe and Linda Evans look good.

Not long after the breakup, Farentino met Deborah Mullowney. Emotionally, he was at a low point, but Deborah's entrance into his life made a difference. When they started sharing a house, he seemed to settle down—at least for a while. Their relationship began to have a real look of permanence. After two failed marriages, Jimmy Farentino surprised everyone, including himself, and turned out to be the domestic type.

"When I first met Jim, I was a slob and didn't even know how to boil an egg," Deborah recalls. "Jim taught me how to clean house and cook. I've even learned how to make pasta from scratch." What had happened to the old Farentino—the ultimate macho man? Where was the card-carrying chauvinist who'd had so much trouble dealing with women's lib (when Michele Lee had begun demanding equal rights at home)? That must have been some other guy. Thanks to Deborah's influence, Farentino had mellowed.

Deborah was busy making casting rounds—and Jimmy gave her his total support. "Other men pretended to like the idea that I was an actress, but couldn't understand my crazy schedule," she remembers. "They'd get angry if I had to call and cancel a date at the last minute because I got stuck at an audition. With Jim, I can call and say, 'Listen, I'll be late,' and he understands. He'll even fix dinner."

With Farentino's encouragement, Deborah's career blossomed. Early in 1982 she won the role of Sloane Denning—a sensuous spider woman—on the brand-new daytime soap *Capitol*. It was a golden opportunity for her. Sloane was slated to be a major character, and Deborah would be surounded by a top-draw cast of Hollywood veterans—Ed Nelson (who'd be playing her father), Rory Calhoun, Richard Egan, Constance Towers, and Carolyn Jones. Those first sweet days on *Capitol* were pure heaven for Deborah: she was learning her craft, starting to get recognition in magazines and gossip columns, and building a career—and a life—of her own.

At first Jimmy didn't mind her twelve-hour working days, but then he was written off *Dynasty*. In the spring of 1982 he left the cast (when Nick Toscanni tried to kill Blake Carrington—an instant death-warrant for any character!) and suddenly he had time on his hands.

In 1983 Farentino worked sporadically and began to brood. In January 1984 he was back on TV with a third series— a police drama called *Blue Thunder*. But the show was a loser and Farentino hated doing it. His growing unhappiness put a strain on his home life and didn't help his reputation in the industry. The word around town wasn't good: Jimmy Farentino was trouble on the set. According to *USA Today* reporter Tom Green, Farentino was "a guy with an attitude problem: cocky, rebellious, volatile, angry, depressed. And an alcoholic."

Jimmy's drinking accelerated rapidly during his stint on *Blue Thunder*, and after the show was canceled he went steadily downhill. *Blue Thunder* had really been a humiliating experience for him. As the hero, Jimmy had top billing—and the scripts were supposed to be built around him—but

Since joining Capitol, *Deborah Mullowney is riding high. Former* Peyton Place *star Ed Nelson plays her father.*

the plots didn't always unravel that way. The real star of the show was a souped-up helicopter that did most of the detective work and made Farentino look like an innocuous second banana. *Blue Thunder* was full of dazzling air stunts and lots of electronic gimmickry, but the scripts didn't have much meat on them for the actors to sink their teeth into.

Going to the studio every day became drudgery, then torture. Farentino spent most of the day sitting in a cramped, uncomfortable chopper that was suspended in the middle of the soundstage. He didn't even have to bother learning his lines—any child could have recited them. The storylines were childish—the dialogue straight from comic books—and the ratings went from bad to worse. Farentino was bored, angry, and frustrated; and after a few weeks, he started smuggling a fifth of vodka onto the set every day and hiding it in the cockpit. It was the only way he could keep going.

Thankfully, ABC canceled the show in September 1984, because by then Farentino was barely functioning on the set. During the last few days of filming he was so drunk he could barely climb out of the helicopter and navigate the walk back to his dressing room.

After the show's demise, things got worse. Deborah was focusing all her energy on *Capitol,* trying not to face the problems at home. She loved

Jimmy, but she wasn't sure she could stick it out. Then, on Thanksgiving Day, the dam burst. At a family dinner, with his mother, son, and Deborah all present, Jimmy finally admitted that he was an alcoholic. He broke down and cried. Then he announced that he was entering a hospital to get treatment.

On the day of her TV wedding, Deborah Mullowney posed with Hollywood vet Richard Egan, who plays her father-in-law. In real life, she married James Farentino in Paris.

Acknowledging his problem was the first step. Getting help was the second. It changed Farentino's life immeasurably and saved his relationship with Deborah Mullowney. Once word of his rehabilitation got out, things began to click for him professionally again. For starters, he was signed to star with Joan Collins in the CBS miniseries *Sins*.

In June 1985, while filming *Sins* in Paris, he decided to mix business with pleasure. Deborah flew over to join him, and they were married in a French civil ceremony. Jimmy's sixteen-year-old son, David, was the best man. The next day Deborah had to return to Los Angeles (to resume work on *Capitol*), but in July she rejoined her new husband on the south coast of France for an extended honeymoon.

In the fall Farentino won the role of Mary Tyler Moore's leading man on her new CBS comedy series, *Mary*. He had to fight to get it. At first Mary didn't want to hear about him. She'd didn't think he was right for the role of the hard-bitten tabloid editor who'd be her boss (and eventually her boyfriend) on the show and had even refused to audition with him. Luckily, she relented because, as it turned out, the chemistry between them was extraordinary.

Unfortunately it couldn't save the show. Despite the inspired casting—and great reviews—*Mary* faltered in the ratings. After only half a season, CBS pulled it off the air, indefinitely, pending massive character and plot changes. Mary Tyler Moore was in seclusion, unavailable for comment. (At the same time that her TV show was failing, her movie, *Such Good Friends,* was taking a terrible beating at the box office.)

If Farentino's future looked glum, the ultimate irony might be that he stood a good chance of running into his ex-wife, Michele Lee, on the neighborhood unemployment line. As the 1985–86 season ended, she was caught up in a bitter contract dispute with *Knots Landing* and threatening not to return next season.

In Hollywood, it seems, men aren't the only hell-raisers.

BACKSTAGE BITCHERY
AND
BLIND AMBITION

Imagine how dull *Knots Landing* would be without Abby (the local adulteress), Karen (the town saint), Lilimae (the Bible-spouting busybody), and Val (the beleaguered wife). No soap opera can survive without 'em—those high-strung heroines and lowdown homewreckers who keep the plots thicker than pea soup. But backstage, too often, is where the real bitchiness begins.

On *Knots Landing* it's a case of three-way rivalry. Joan Van Ark plays Val Ewing Gibson, the show's original heroine, but she's often overshadowed in popularity by Michele Lee, who plays Val's savvy and self-righteous neighbor, Karen Fairgate MacKenzie. And when it comes to sheer bedroom statistics, they both take a back seat to blonde bombshell Donna Mills (Abby).

In the spring of 1986 the rivalry had reached such a pitch that Michele Lee almost packed her bags and quit. When the season cliff-hanger was filmed, her new contract was still unsigned. Just in case she wouldn't be returning in the fall, the writers engineered a mysterious disappearance for Karen, leaving the door open to kill her off. If that happened, only the audience would have mourned. Some of the show's other regulars probably would have danced with glee.

What did Michele have to grouse about? According to castmates, who resented her frequent feistiness and Queen-Bee presence on the set, nothing at all. But according to Michele—and astute viewers of *Knots Landing*—things were plenty wrong. Her character was suffering from the worst kind of soap opera affliction: terminal happiness. She was stuck in a rut with no way out—the noblest woman in town married to Kevin Dobson (Mac), the noblest man. Karen had already survived everything—widowhood, drug dependency, an assassin's bullet, even a chemical-waste spill. And every time the show tried to derail her domestic life, viewers balked. Meanwhile, during the last two years, Joan Van Ark, Donna Mills, and a newcomer named Lisa Hartman (who wore the tightest pants and skimpiest blouses on TV) had dominated the action, much to Michele's chagrin. As one insider commented, "To some people it seemed like the show cares more about Donna's eye makeup and Lisa's cleavage than it does about Michele's storyline. But they're the sexpots—and Michele's the saint—and we all know where the ratings are. Besides, it's much easier to write for bad characters than good ones."

Ultimately, Lorimar did come to terms with Michele Lee (a bigger salary and the promise of a few storyline changes helped), but that doesn't mean tensions will ease up backstage. The cold-shoulder treatment's been going on since the show started. Michele's first rival was Joan Van Ark. When *Knots Landing* premiered in December 1979—as a direct spin-off of *Dallas*—the two central characters were supposed to be Val Ewing and her husband Gary (Ted Shackelford), who'd left Southfork to start a new life together in California. But smart, gutsy Karen soon emerged as the real heroine, while Val turned into the show's biggest victim. In 1981 Michele lost her TV husband, Don Murray (who left in a heated contract dispute), but a year later she got a new, younger leading man—actor Kevin Dobson. Michele also won a coveted best-actress Emmy nomination, while Joan Van Ark didn't.

In script after script, Karen got to tilt at windmills, take on the mob, tackle the government, and dry everybody else's tears. Val, meanwhile, was next door busy getting dumped on by her drunken husband and browbeaten by her nagging mother. Finally, as a sop to Joan Van Ark, who was increasingly disturbed about her character's near catatonic passivity, the writers transformed Val from a high-school dropout into a bestselling novelist overnight. In 1983 she also got a more boyish leading man—actor Doug Sheehan—and no attempt was made to bring Charlene Tilton over from *Dallas*. Charlene played Val's grown daughter, Lucy, and her presence on *Knots Landing* would have constantly underlined the fact that Joan Van Ark was hardly a girlish belle anymore.

Meanwhile other backstage inequities rankled. Dobson, Shackelford, and Sheehan all felt that their characters were being slowly emasculated because the show's writers were too women-oriented. (Are the women on *Knots Landing* stronger than the men? Take a case in point: Karen—

not Mac or Gary or Ben—solved the mystery of Val's kidnapped twins.) The 1984 arrival of Ava Gardner—as William Devane's barracuda mother—posed other problems. Ava was only a guest star, doing a handful of episodes, but her presence dominated every script. She was given a sharper storyline—and more scenes—than Julie Harris (Val's mother) who was a longtime regular. "They were dazzled by the fact that Ava was a former glamour queen," one setsider claims. "It didn't matter that Julie Harris is

Getting away from the tensions of Knots Landing, *Donna Mills paints the town with longtime friend* Capitol *producer John Conboy and* Newhart's *Mary Frann.*

probably the greatest stage actress in America, that she's won five Tony awards, an unheard-of achievement, and that she could act rings around Ava Gardner if given half a chance. All the prime-time soaps have movie-star-itis. The same thing happened when Lana Turner and Gina Lollo-brigida came on *Falcon Crest*. The producers practically handed over the show to them."

These days possibly the only happy actress on *Knots Landing* is Donna Mills—and why not? Her latest costar, Hunt Block (Peter), who's still under thirty, is the youngest leading man of all. But the tensions on *Knots Landing* are nothing compared to the fireworks that periodically flare backstage at another Lorimar production, *Falcon Crest*. Most of the heat is generated by the show's most explosive star, Jane Wyman.

In the spring of 1982—at the end of the show's first shaky season on the air—Lana Turner was brought on to raise the ratings. There was so much advance publicity that the ploy worked. Viewers eagerly turned in to watch her character, mild-mannered Jacqueline Perrault, trade barbs with Angela Channing, the toughest old broad in the Tuscany Valley. But Jane didn't think there was room for two movie queens on the same set. She considered *Falcon Crest* strictly her turf—and she intended to keep it that way. Besides, Lana Turner was hardly a bosom buddy. Their feud harked all the way back to their starlet days at Warner Brothers.

In 1939, seventeen-year-old, curvaceous Lana had nearly wrecked Jane's budding romance with Ronald Reagan. Even though her dates with Reagan were stricly prearranged publicity outings, the photos that appeared in newspapers angered Jane. Later on, even after Jane became Mrs. Ronald Reagan, the rivalry continued. All through the 1940s the two actresses competed for public attention. Jane may have won the Oscar for her serious dramatic work in *Johnny Belinda,* but Lana achieved something that Jane still coveted—grass-roots popularity. Lana was a top-ten draw at the box office; Jane was not.

Now, thirty years later on *Falcon Crest,* the situation was reversed—Jane was the star and Lana was merely the guest. Robert Foxworth, Susan Sullivan, and all the other regulars had to acknowledge the fact that, as one cameraman put it, "When you work with Jane, you dance to her tune." But Lana Turner wasn't in the business of dancing to anyone's tune. And when the producers brought her back for a second season, Lana began to think of herself as the show's salvation and to make imperious demands. The set had to be closed to visitors whenever she was working. Her dressing room had to be the same size as Jane Wyman's. A limousine had to pick her up every morning.

Every actor on *Falcon Crest* had a setside chair with his or her name

Jane Wyman rules the roost, on set and off, on Falcon Crest.

on it. Lana ordered the propman to have hers repainted. Instead of just "Lana Turner," it had to say "*Miss* Lana Turner." Jane Wyman took one look and requested that her own chair be moved as far away as possible from Lana's. The final blow-up came when Jane was off the set for a few days and Lana decided to take over. She began insisting that everyone wear *Falcon Crest* badges because she was worried about strangers sneaking on the set (she was obsessed with security). The show acquiesed. A few days later, when Jane Wyman returned to work, the studio guard wouldn't let her in because she had no badge. Jane brushed past them, stormed onto the set, and began ripping off the badges of every crew member she encountered. "This is my show. I don't need a badge!" she shrieked. Then there was total silence. "You could hear a pin drop in the studio after that one," an observer commented.

From that point on Jane Wyman and Lana Turner never spoke unless the script required them to do so. To pacify Jane, Lana's character became progressively more villainous and was eventually killed off. To keep tensions to a minimum, Lana's death script was written in such a way that she and Jane never appeared on-screen together. Even though Jacqueline Perrault was shot at a wedding which took place at Angela's house, the

Top: *Jane Wyman was one of the first film stars to make the transition to TV. In 1961 she guested on Sebastian Cabot's show,* Checkmate. Bottom: *Following her Hollywood decline, Lana Turner appeared in such unsuccessful movies as* Bittersweet Love. Falcon Crest *marked a tempestuous comeback for her.*

characters never actually stood face to face. Lana's part of the scene was filmed separately, then spliced in, so that she and Jane Wyman could work on different days and avoid all contact.

Had Lorimar forced these aging vixens to keep working together, it's possible that a setside slugfest might have broken out. It wouldn't have been the first one. In 1980 two *Days of Our Lives* actresses—Susan Hayes and Brenda Benet—actually had to be pulled apart when they came to blows during a tense rehearsal. The object of their quarrel was Susan's real-life husband, Bill, who happened to play Brenda's lover on the show.

The feud became public knowledge when Brenda threatened to take Susan to court on an assault charge, alleging that Susan had walloped her in the mouth with a purse. But Susan told the press, "The accident occurred during a scene. Brenda charged that blood flowed from her lip, but if I'd

Bill and Susan Hayes, married in real life, sometimes found it difficult working together on Days of Our Lives.

swung so hard, how come my husband Bill, who was standing right there, wasn't hurt? Brenda also claimed that my language toward her was abusive, but how can that be when we don't speak to each other?"

Executive Producer Al Rabin convinced Brenda to abandon her lawsuit, and six months later she and Susan actually patched up their differences. By that time, though, Brenda was becoming increasingly erratic, and her emotional instability was apparent to the whole cast. In 1982 she took her own life.

As for Susan Hayes, she still has occasional flashes of temper on the set (she now works on *Young and Restless),* but husband Bill has learned to go with the flow. "Susan is very emotional and reacts immediately," he says, "yet I don't want her to change and be somebody she's not. I fell in love with the girl just as she was, so why change her?"

Still and all, not every soap opera prima donna, no matter how much her territory is threatened, has fangs. *All My Children*'s Susan Lucci is a model of sweetness and light off-screen—she saves her tears for the privacy of her own dressing room. With her shy manner and little-girl voice, it's hard to believe she's one of the most powerful stars in daytime television.

Somehow Susan seems to pull it all off. After sixteen years of playing high-fashion harridan Erica Kane, Susan's still married to the same man (Austrian-born hotel exec Helmut Huber) and she seems content pruning rose bushes, raising their two children—Liza, eleven; and Andreas, six— and searching for armoires and armchairs for their magificent Tudor mansion in a secluded Long Island suburb. There's never been a hint of scandal linking her with any of her many leading men. But her ambition and frustrations . . . well, that's another story.

She's never won an Emmy, despite the fact that she's been nominated seven times, more than any other actress in a daytime drama. It may be that her performance is just a bit too campy—or maybe the blue-ribbon panel of judges that hands out the Emmies every year figures that her $500,000-plus salary is reward enough. Susan's lost to some very distinguished adversaries, including Judith Light (of *Who's the Boss?* fame) who garnered two Emmies in a row for playing prostitute Karen Wolek on *One Life to Live.* But Susan broke down and cried at the awards ceremonies only once—in 1983 when castmate Dorothy Lyman stole the victory right out of her hands.

Lyman's rise to fame on *All My Children* was truly spectacular. She arrived on the show in 1981 (in a supporting role) and engineered her way to the top in two short years. Her character, Opal Gardner, was originally slated to be a mean, money-hungry lowlife, but Dorothy took

Susan Lucci gets a lift from costar Jean LeClerc—in a hot romantic interlude from All My Children.

the scripts and turned them upside down. She invented her own wardrobe—spandex pants and hot-pink halter tops—and wrote her own dialogue, some of it the most hilarious material ever uttered on a daytime drama. The audience was supposed to want to wring her neck, but pretty soon they were cheering her on—especially when she brazenly told Erica Kane exactly where to shove her chic designer outfits. Until Opal's tacky arrival, Susan Lucci had had the market cornered on soap-opera camp. Now Dorothy Lyman was getting all the laughs—and Susan wasn't very happy about playing straight woman to this loudmouthed upstart.

As Dorothy's popularity mushroomed, backstage cordiality dipped to an icy low. Susan wasn't the only veteran who began to feel cramped by Dorothy's brassy style. The writers adored Opal ad nauseam because this bleached-blond airhead was such a hoot. They kept writing reams of cutesy, cornpone dialogue and clever plot inventions for her, while other stars and storylines were shunted aside. Disgruntled castmates snidely

Dressed as tacky temptress Opal Gardner, Dorothy Lyman scored a major hit on All My Children. *(With castmate Michael Minor.)*

referred to *All My Children* as "The Opal Gardner Hour" and "Dorothy Does Daytime."

From the outset it didn't seem likely that Dorothy and Susan would become backstage sorority sisters. They did socialize occasionally—Dorothy and her boyfriend Vincent Malle attended Susan's 1982 at-home Oscar party—but generally their paths didn't cross. Susan's off-screen life, based totally in Long Island, revolved around her husband and kids. Dorothy's first priority was her career—domesticity was hardly her strong suit.

Dorothy's marriage to Broadway director John Tillinger had produced two children. When her daughter, Emma, was five, and her son, Sebastian, was three, Dorothy had walked out. Although she and John agreed on joint custody, the children remained with their father in Connecticut, while Dorothy moved into a Manhattan bachelor-girl flat. The children visited her on weekends, but Dorothy was now free to pursue her career with a white-hot zeal that full-time motherhood didn't permit. Some people were aghast at what she'd done—others felt it took guts.

A year and a half after the divorce, Dorothy admitted, "It's certainly an unpopular feminine choice and it was an extremely difficult one for me. . . . Living alone and not being a mother anymore day to day was an enormous shock. It was very painful, especially when people would hear that I had two children and they weren't with me."

Despite her outward bravado, Dorothy was haunted by a deep sense of loss. She preferred seeing the children in Manhattan, not at the Tillinger house. Trips back to Connecticut meant too many confrontations with the past. During one visit, while out walking with the children, Dorothy broke down. "I was just overwhelmed by an awful sense of sadness and loss," she recalled. "I sat down on a rock and started to cry, and I don't really do that in front of my children very often."

But she had few regrets about discarding the marriage itself. The seeds of the breakup had been there from the very beginning, she claimed. "I was never really interested in getting married," she said. "I was pregnant at the time, so I succumbed to family pressures. We were certainly in love, but the pregnancy changed our relationship. We were suddenly forced to create a family situation."

Eventually Dorothy felt so suffocated by the day-to-day drudgery of the domestic grind—and life in suburban Connecticut—that she had to get out. She felt that her children would do better staying on in Connecticut, where all their attachments were, but she needed to be back in Manhattan, closer to the hub of things. During her marriage to Tillinger, Dorothy had appeared on three soap operas—*A World Apart, Edge of*

To the public, the All My Children *cast was one big happy family (l-r): Susan Lucci, Dorothy Lyman, Larry Lau, and Ruth Warrick.*

Night, and *Another World*—but now she began to broaden her horizons. She blossomed as a businesswoman as well as an actress. For starters, she produced and played a lead role in the long-running off-Broadway comedy, *A Coupla White Chicks Sitting Around Talking.* Then, three years after her divorce, came her pivotal role on *All My Children,* which turned out to be her ticket to Hollywood.

Comedy on daytime television is so rare that Dorothy's stint as Opal Gardner stood out like a diamond in a haystack. But was she really all that sensational—or just an overrated oddball? It was galling—to some people at least—to watch her walk off with two consecutive Emmies (best supporting actress, 1982; best actress, 1983) for a performance that was more like slapstick than true soap opera. Her detractors argued that Opal really belonged in a Carol Burnett skit and—ironically enough—that's exactly where she wound up. Even before her contract was up on *All My Children,* she landed on the *Carol Burnett Show* spin-off, *Mama's Family,* playing Ken Berry's wife. Her new prime-time incarnation, Naomi Oates Harper, was practically the spitting image of Opal Gardner—most of the dialogue could have come right off the pages of an *All My Children* script.

Dorothy's jump into prime-time must have rankled Susan Lucci, especially since Susan has been paying her dues in daytime for sixteen years.

No matter how much *All My Children* keeps sweetening the pot, Susan can't help but feel claustrophobic from time to time. In 1980 NBC almost lured her away, but not to Hollywood. They came close to hijacking her onto one of their New York soaps—*Another World* or *Texas*—by offering her a record sum of money and the chance to create a screen persona who'd be totally different than Erica. But ABC held on to Susan by giving her $240,000 a year (at that time a new high) and the promise of showcase roles in three prime-time movies.

Is it money that ultimately keeps her from leaving?—or loyalty?—or sheer fear of the unknown? *All My Children* is practically the only acting job Susan's ever held. She seems rooted to the place, no matter what— and things haven't always been a bed of roses. Even after a dangerous backstage accident in 1978, Susan didn't seriously think about quitting.

The accident—one of the most bizarre mishaps in studio history— happened during a rehearsal break. Susan had gone to the wardrobe room to pick out a new hat for a particularly glitzy scene she was doing that day. All the hats were stocked on a high shelf near the ceiling. There was no wardrobe mistress in sight, and Susan (who's not much taller than five feet) wasn't really concentrating on where she was going. She was too busy staring straight up at that shelf—wondering how she was going to get at those hats. That's when she took an eight-foot fall through a trap door in the floor. The door had been left open by some electricians who'd gone to lunch; they were working on underground cables that lay directly below the wardrobe room.

Susan was badly bruised and shaken. Luckily, her screams brought help quickly, though it took a long time to calm her down and several weeks for the swelling on her legs to go down. She insisted on finishing that day's taping, but had to miss several days of work after that because she couldn't walk the flight of stairs from the set to her dressing room.

Another star might have considered a lawsuit. Susan figured that she was lucky enough to escape without a concussion or any broken bones, and decided to forget about it.

Meanwhile—after her near-mutiny in 1980—ABC kept good on its promise of prime-time roles. But she never became a regular on a nighttime series as Dorothy Lyman did. Susan guested on *Fantasy Island* and starred in two made-for-TV movies, *Invitation to Hell* and *Mafia Princess*. In the first she played the devil (disguised as a California country club director). In the second, which turned out to be a real blockbuster in the ratings, she was cast as the daughter of notorious crime lord Sam Giancana (played by Tony Curtis).

But other attempts to break away from her "Erica Kane" image haven't exactly set off fireworks. So far, since 1970, Susan's only appeared in one feature film, doing a cameo in the *Airplane*-style comedy, *Young Doctors in Love;* and her record debut on a quickly forgotten LP featuring half a dozen ABC soap stars didn't make Madonna lose any sleep.

In 1985 reports circulated that Susan would dump *All My Children* to join *Dallas.* ABC denied that an offer from Lorimar had even taken place, but the rumors refused to die. And it seemed to make sense. With Patrick Duffy leaving the show, it was no secret that the producers were anxious to add as much new glitter as possible to the Southfork scene. One of Susan's former *AMC* costars, Dack Rambo, was already playing Jack Ewing, and she could have easily segued onto *Dallas* as a possible love interest for him. There was another option, too. Susan would have been dazzling as Angelica Nero—the malevolent Greek tycoon who nearly outfoxed J.R.—a plum that eventually went to Barbara Carrera.

But even if *Dallas* did make overtures, Susan probably wasn't all that anxious to bite. After all, ABC wasn't treating her badly. She already had *Mafia Princess* on the horizon, and with Dorothy Lyman out of her hair in Pine Valley, Susan was once more the show's uncontested queen of camp—and star vamp.

Some setsiders doubt she'll ever leave. With her husband and children firmly entrenched on the East Coast, a permanent move to Hollywood would mean a family upheaval. *All My Children* is still anxious to hang on to her and keeps fattening her bank account with every new contract. "Besides, I don't want to play some detective's girlfriend or wisecracking receptionist on prime-time," Susan once said. "I'd never leave *All My Children* for that."

"She's really waiting for Joan Collins to ditch *Dynasty*," jokes one backstage crony. "I wouldn't be surprised if ABC already has a script in some secret vault. Sure, can't you just see it? Alexis Carrington gets blown up in an explosion. She needs extensive plastic surgery. When she wakes up in the hospital and the bandages come off—voilà!—it's Susan Lucci! And what a gold mine for *Dynasty*. Susan's young enough to be Joan Collins's daughter. She won't even need her first face-lift for another twenty years!"

To Joan Collins fans, such a scenario might be a real nightmare. Come to think of it, it might be a nightmare for Susan, too, especially if she woke up in that hospital room and found out Dorothy Lyman was playing her nurse.

BLOOD
MONEY

*E*arthquakes devastate the Tuscany Valley; fires nearly destroy Southfork; and Moldavia may not be the safest place to hold a royal wedding (just ask the machine-gun-crazed cast of *Dynasty*). But on-screen bloodbaths are sometimes mild compared with the vicious sniping that goes on regularly behind the scenes.

The soap world is a pressure cooker. The stakes are high—and when push comes to shove, most actors, writers, and producers are all too willing to roll up their sleeves, bare their claws, and go for the jugular.

Larry Hagman's long-running feud with his *Dallas* boss, Phil Capice, is legendary. When Capice quit his executive producer post in the spring of 1986, Hagman publicly ridiculed him as "no-talented" and "obnoxious." A cheap shot? In Hollywood, Capice is generally considered one of television's most competent and civilized producers. Hagman, too, is regarded as a genuinely peace-loving man. All-out war seems distinctly out of character for them both. Yet war it's been ever since Larry went on strike—and nearly sabotaged production—six years ago. That was their first skirmish, and it escalated very quickly into a full-blown conflict.

Let's go back to the summer of 1980 when J. R. had just been shot and America was starting to go *Dallas* crazy. Out of nowhere, Larry Hagman suddenly mushroomed into a matinee (and merchandising) idol. Like any smart businessman he realized it was the perfect time to renegotiate his contract. He had the world by its proverbial tail. But CBS, Lorimar, and Phil Capice somehow weren't aware of that, or at least they coolly feigned innocence and turned up their collective noses at Hagman's demands. So Larry went on strike. He literally left the show—and left California—refusing to return to work unless he got a hefty salary raise.

It was the first time that Lorimar and Phil Capice had to deal head-on with the new, improved Larry Hagman—Larry the megastar. His ego had been swelling by leaps and bounds ever since the airing of the season's cliff-hanger on March 21, 1980.

When J. R. was gunned down by an unknown assailant, Larry knocked Alan Alda out of the top slot as America's favorite male TV star. "All of a sudden at forty-nine I'm a sex symbol," Larry later confided to *TV Guide*. "All well and good. CBS was making a bundle. Lorimar, the production company, was feeling no pain either. Me? The guys peddling the T-shirts with my face on them were probably doing better than I was."

On June 12, 1980, the first day of shooting for the new season, Larry was conspicuously absent from the set. He was, in fact, lollygagging in London—six thousand miles from Lorimar's L.A. studios—flaunting his bad-boy, let's-play-hooky behavior by grinning for the Fleet Street paparazzi while he toured Madame Tussaud's Wax Museum. While Hagman fiddled, Lorimar burned—and then retaliated. Capice's first move was to start negotiating with Robert Culp to replace Hagman as J. R. With his strong TV credits—*I Spy* and *The Greatest American Hero*—Culp was (hopefully) a big enough name to fill the gap, yet he wouldn't cost the show an arm and a leg per episode.

Capice's second move was to pave the way in storyline terms for a possible Culp takeover. As production began on the new season with Hagman's future still up in the air, J. R.'s post-gunshot fate also remained purposely vague. At first J. R. was played by an unknown actor, a double, with his face completely wrapped in bandages. The scripts began hinting that J. R. might require extensive plastic surgery. That gimmick, of course, was to smooth over Culp's possible arrival: it would have easily explained the fact that Culp bore no resemblance at all to his much rounder-faced, less handsome predecessor.

During those sultry June days—while Hagman nonchalantly sipped champagne and checked out the thoroughbreds at Ascot, then moved on to the Bahamas for some gambling at Paradise Island—the wheels of contract wizardry ground exceedingly slowly. For a time it did look as if he might have overplayed his hand. True, Hagman was holding some rather high cards—his enormous viewer popularity was worth a couple of aces—but other high-rollers like Farrah Fawcett (*Charlie's Angels*) and Suzanne Somers (*Three's Company*) had tried the same holdout tactics before, only to find themselves left out in the cold. Hagman acknowledged the fact that he was locked into a "dangerous game," but he was fully prepared to go to the limit. And Lorimar knew that. They also knew that he was too valuable to lose. And perhaps, the only alternative—replacing him—was just too damned risky. *Dallas* had never recast a major role before; they had no way of gauging viewer reaction. Would the public accept a new J. R., or turn away in droves? Ultimately, *Dallas* couldn't risk finding out. After ten sweltering days, Lorimar gave in to Hagman's sky-high financial demands. And agreed to pay him a whopping $75,000 per episode (an unprecedented amount for a prime-time soaper).

Hagman's costars—Linda Gray, Patrick Duffy, and Victoria Principal—were all secretly cheering him on, and for good reason. His victory would undoubtedly mean future salary raises for them, too. But the backstage brass came off the battlefield still licking their wounds. It boiled down to this: an actor had gained ground; therefore, the producers had lost some. For the next six years the situation continued to deteriorate.

In 1980 Larry Hagman became the highest-paid star on a prime-time soap, and his public appearances at places like Opryland drew record crowds.

Hagman frequently made unasked-for storyline suggestions, not all of which were appreciated by the writers and producers. Even when certain plot twists eventually did find their way onto the screen, the question of credit was sometimes disputed. A case in point: the revelation that Ray Krebbs was really Jock Ewing's illegitimate son. According to Steve Kanaly, who plays Ray, that story idea came out of an innocent offset conversation. "Larry Hagman and I were standing around one day," Kanaly recalls, "and Larry looked at Patrick Duffy and Jim Davis (who played Jock). Then he turned to me and suddenly said, 'You know, Steve, you look more like you could be Jim's son than any of us.' Well, a light went on—Larry and I got the idea at the same exact moment—and we ran right to the producers with it."

Shortly afterward the writers began planting the seeds for Ray's eventual Ewingization. Nevertheless, Phil Capice later denied that either Kanaly or Hagman had ever volunteered any input regarding that storyline. According to Capice, the show's writers had long been toying with the idea of developing a fuller life for Ray, of transforming him from the outcast ranch foreman into a more sympathetic figure. Making him an instant Ewing, which bound him closer to the other main characters—was the way they chose to do it. Capice maintains that they would have gone the same route with Ray, even if Steve Kanaly had red hair and freckles and Jim Davis had been dark-haired and olive-skinned.

He pooh-poohs the notion that anyone on the set ever noticed a strong physical resemblance between Kanaly and Davis. As further proof that the producers, not Hagman, always had Kanaly's best interests at heart, he mentions that Susan Howard (Donna) was originally brought on as a new love interest for Ken Kercheval (Cliff)—there was even a brief, early reference to the fact that Cliff and Donna were old college classmates—but viewers never saw that relationship develop. Capice and company decided to save her for a major involvement with Kanaly instead—another example of their dedication to expanding Kanaly's role on the show.

Perhaps Larry Hagman actually made storyline contributions to the show; perhaps not. But over the years his power backstage definitely increased. He was responsible for cigarette smoking being banned on the set. He fought to get Linda Gray a shot at directing one episode. Each season he directed several episodes himself. And he became a kind of one-man actors' union, often championing other people's grievances. According to Linda Gray, if someone was having trouble with the wardrobe or makeup department, if they wanted a line change in the script, he or she frequently bypassed the producers' office and went directly to Larry. He had a reputation for getting things done.

In the actors' eyes, Larry became more and more of a hero. "We all adore him," says Pat Colbert, who plays Dora Mae, the hostess at the Oil Barons Club. "He and Patrick Duffy keep us in stitches during rehearsal. They're our life perservers when things get tense." On one not-so-funny occasion, though, during the filming of a restaurant scene, Larry noticed that an extra had started to choke on a piece of food. "The rest of us had

Larry Hagman first achieved TV fame on I Dream of Jeannie *with Barbara Eden.*

our backs turned, so Larry was the only one who really saw what was happening," recalls Pat. "He didn't waste a second. He rushed over and performed the Heimlich maneuver. In a matter of seconds he saved that man's life."

As Hagman's stock rose on the set, Capice's seemed to decline. His unsuccessful attempt to foist Donna Reed on the cast—as the new Miss Ellie—only exacerbated the situation.

In the spring of 1983, sixty-year-old Barbara Bel Geddes—the show's original Miss Ellie—began to be plagued by heart problems. She finished out the season—barely—and five days after shooting her last scenes underwent triple bypass surgery at Cedars-Sinai Medical Center in Los Angeles. She returned to *Dallas* the following fall, but her workload had to be considerably lightened and she missed several episodes in September and October while she was still convalescing. (The writers explained her sudden absence by sending Miss Ellie on a long trip to Galveston.) Barbara finished out that season, but then chose to leave permanently. She announced that she was retiring from the grind of weekly television for the sake of her health.

Dallas was now confronted with a prickly dilemma: how to handle her departure. The producers created a dark scenario to explain her absence (they could quietly pull the plug on Miss Ellie) and a lighter one (they could send her off on an endless world cruise with her bridegroom, Clayton Farlow). Death or disappearance—the devil or the deep blue sea—neither option made much sense.

In 1981 *Dallas* had faced the death of actor Jim Davis by killing off his character, too. But with Jock Ewing, the patriarch of the clan, gone, terminating Miss Ellie seemed out of the question. The show couldn't survive with both parental figures gone.

"We didn't want to leave J. R. an orphan," explains Capice. "When Jim Davis died, there was so much publicity surrounding his death, and he was so identified with the character of Jock Ewing, that there was never any question of replacing him. Out of respect to Jim's memory, we felt it would be wrong to bring in another actor. Besides, we still had Miss Ellie fulfilling that very important parental role of keeping J. R. in line.

"However, Barbara's leaving was a far different situation. We couldn't simply eliminate Miss Ellie—she was the only authority figure left at Southfork—it would have changed the whole chemistry of the show. Without mama around, J. R. would have started running wild. Family devotion—to his mother, to his son—that's what redeems him. So even though we were concerned that the audience might not suspend its disbelief and accept a new actress in the role, it was the only option open to us. We had no good solution to the problem of Barbara Bel Geddes leaving; we just felt recasting was the lesser of two evils."

And so Donna Reed, who had starred in her own TV sitcom, *The Donna Reed Show,* for eight seasons, was persuaded to step in. She joined the show several weeks into the 1984–85 season—with an avalanche of preparatory hype in all the supermarket tabloids—but viewers just didn't warm up to her. There were also reports that Larry Hagman, who'd supposedly campaigned for his own mother, Mary Martin (a genuine Texan), to take over the role, gave Donna only a lukewarm reception on the set. All in all it was a difficult season for her. In her attempt not to copy Barbara Bel Geddes' performance, she created a Miss Ellie who seemed to come from a much more rarefied atmosphere than the rest of the Ewings. Donna's version of Miss Ellie was a gracious Southfork matron, well-bred and distinctly upper crust. It was hard to believe she'd ever roped cattle and branded steers at her daddy's side.

Her success on *Dallas* seemed dubious at best, but other changes virtually signed her pink slip. In the spring of 1985 two other cast members—Charlene Tilton and Patrick Duffy— decided to jump ship. In the light of those defections, Lorimar felt it was imperative to get Barbara Bel Geddes back. Even though Donna Reed had signed a four-year contract, the show hastily bought her out, but reportedly handled her dismissal in a less than tactful way. (She got word that she'd been dumped from the show while on vacation in Europe, with no prior warning from the producers.)

Meanwhile Larry Hagman and Linda Gray, two of Barbara's closest pals in the cast, phoned her at her sixty-acre farm in upstate New York and helped convince her to return. After a year off, she was in much better physical condition and, obviously, the charm of permanent retirement wore off pretty quickly. As far as returning went, more money wasn't an issue, but her health was. So Barbara's new contract exempted her from doing any location shooting in Dallas during June and July, the two hottest months of the year.

After spending most of her year-long retirement just relaxing at her farm, Barbara was more than anxious to get back to work. But the crossfire over Donna Reed's dismissal disturbed her. "I think the way she was told was very unfortunate," Barbara confided to a national tabloid. "You would have thought the producers could have discussed it with her before she went on vacation."

Donna herself was angry enough to institute a lawsuit against her former bosses, but her war with *Dallas* proved futile. Just a few months after leaving the show, she was stricken with cancer and died before the year was out.

Donna Reed's death—and the backstage maneuvering surrounding Barbara Bel Geddes's return—weren't the only shadows hanging over the Southfork set. The dawn of the 1985–86 season—without Patrick Duffy— left the show minus a strong romantic leading man. Suddenly, life at Southfork seemed lackluster and vapid, and the ratings soon began to reflect it. *Dallas* tried to introduce new characters and storylines, but the public balked. Dack Rambo, who played a tall, dark, and handsome Ewing cousin, Jack, was supposed to take viewers' minds off Patrick Duffy. It didn't work. Neither did some of the show's other hastily concocted ploys— like the resurrection of Pam's old lover Mark Graison (John Beck) or Sue Ellen's umpteenth bout with alcoholism.

Barbara Carrera came on—dressed to the nines and dripping with venom—as a new match for J. R. Her character, Angelica Nero, was part Joan Collins, part Dragon Lady—but somehow her exotic Mediterranean style seemed bizarrely out of place on the dusty Southfork landscape. "It was like running into Eva Peron at a Sunday barbecue," one setsider sniped. "You kept wondering if she'd poisoned the A-1 Sauce!"

All through the show's declining eighth season, Hagman and Capice fought over the show's new touches. Hagman, with much support from other cast members, argued that the writers were veering too far away from family squabbles and star-crossed love—*Dallas'* real strengths—in favor of James Bond–type adventure. And it wasn't keeping viewers hooked. Certainly, this season, the Ewings and the Barneses were doing more globe-trotting than ever before. There was a dazzling emerald-mine expedition to Venezuela and a Greek assassination plot against J. R., aboard an Onassis-style yacht, but despite those storyline pyrotechnics ratings continued to slide.

The tabloids asserted that one daring storyline never even made it to the air. Originally, Barbara Carrera was supposed to be involved in a lesbian relationship with her female assistant (played by Merete Van Kamp), but Larry Hagman, Susan Howard (who's a born-again Christian), and Barbara Bel Geddes all threatened to walk if that storyline was actually played out. They were adamant about keeping *Dallas* a family-oriented show—and they ultimately got their way.

By the end of the season, Carrera and Van Kamp were both gone—and the show was making a strong effort to return to its roots. In an even more surprising development, Patrick Duffy was back (after he lost the lead in another TV series, *Heart of the City*), and Hagman couldn't have been more delighted about his TV brother's return. He'd predicted that Duffy wouldn't stay away forever, and he'd been proven right on another count, too—exotic storylines didn't work on *Dallas*.

Hagman also got his way as far as Phil Capice was concerned. Tired of haggling with the show's temperamental stars and constantly worrying over ebbing ratings, Capice finally bowed out and Leonard Katzman (who enjoyed a much smoother relationship with Hagman) became the new executive producer.

■　　■　　■

Dallas isn't the only war zone in the soap world. Larry Hagman and Phil Capice could visit any daytime serial set and feel right at home.

Days of Our Lives is a constant hotbed of tension, and has been for some time. In the late 1970s head writer Pat Falken-Smith left in a heated contract dispute and sued NBC, Corday Productions, and Columbia Pictues TV (the show's joint owners) for several million dollars. She then segued over to *General Hospital*, turned Luke Spencer's rape of Laura Baldwin into the sexiest romance in soap history, and pushed *GH* to the top of the ratings. But Pat also fought bitterly with her bosses at ABC, and left that show in a huff, too. So pretty soon it was kiss and make up with the Corday and Columbia execs, and Pat returned to *Days of Our Lives*. But her reconciliation lasted about as long as a commercial break. She was sitting in her office, being interviewed by the editor of a daytime fan magazine, when Pat got the fatal phone call—she was being fired for the second time. The producers wanted her to clear out by the end of the day. Pat was stunned, and so was the embarrassed young editor who sat there watching this horrifying drama unfold. The subject of the interview, ironically enough, had been Pat's successful return to *Days of Our Lives*.

Josh Taylor also cried foul play when he left the show in 1981. After four years of playing macho construction worker Chris Kositchek, Josh felt his character was getting shafted. For months he'd never appeared on the show more than twice a week, and then only as a back-burner character, even though every popularity poll ranked him as one of the show's hottest assets. When he gave notice, the writers didn't even bother to give Chris an interesting farewell scene—they just sent him off to live on a farm "somewhere in the country." For Josh, it was the ultimate insult. "I felt like I was being put to pasture," he recalls.

He was also being sent to the poorhouse—and he set up a real public wail about it. In magazine interviews, Josh alleged that *Days* owed him thousands of dollars in back pay for not using him in enough episodes. *Days* claimed otherwise. Josh considered a lawsuit, then dropped the idea. But he didn't hide his anger from the press. "Whenever I hear someone mention *Days of Our Lives* now, I want to cringe," he said. He regretted that he'd gone out of his way to make things easier for the show's writers by giving notice months before his contract was up. "I feel like a fool for showing some class," he said. "Being nice cost me a lot of money, and knowing all that has to change you. I live a block away from the studio and had planned to visit, but I don't want any more reminders of the pettiness now. I don't even want to watch *Days of Our Lives* anymore."

Josh's statement that being nice cost him a lot of money referred to the fact that once the writers knew he was leaving, they refused to create any more storyline for him. That's why he was so underused during his last few months on the show. If he'd been more ruthless about it, he could have pretended that he intended to re-sign and then left *Days* in the lurch with a half-started story that some other actor would have had to finish. From Josh's point of view, his considerateness was hardly repaid in kind, and even executive producer Al Rabin conceded that Josh may have had a legitimate "moral complaint" against the show.

But soap opera—like politics—makes strange bedfellows—just one year later Josh Taylor was back, and suddenly vowing eternal loyalty. Apparently, in the interim, he'd learned some hard lessons about life outside the safety of the soap opera cocoon. His first attempt at prime-time stardom—a police series called *Riker*—lasted exactly one month on the air. His low-budget movie, *Waltz Across Texas,* didn't generate much momentum either. Meanwhile, *Days* lured him back with a lucrative new contract—and the promise of better scripts. "They

Josh Taylor almost took Days of Our Lives *to court, but Josh (who's a former attorney) later changed his mind.*

also told me how much they wanted me back, and that smoothed over a lot of the hard feelings," he said. "No matter how you slice it, for an actor in this business, it's nice to be wanted." (In 1986, Josh became Valerie Harper's co-star in her new sit-com, *Valerie,* but this time he didn't chuck daytime; instead he juggled both shooting schedules. He's been burned enough times to know that the only thing tangible in show business is that script in your hand and that paycheck in your pocket.)

When it comes to getting burned, a die-hard New Jersey fan named Diane Grusenski claims she's got the market cornered, thanks to the infuriating treatment she received from the cast and brass of *Days of Our Lives.* For three years she's been president of the Hour Glass Fan Club, a national organization of viewers united in their undying devotion to *Days.* During Christmas week of 1985, Diane organized a fan club luncheon in Paramus, New Jersey, and convinced several of the show's stars—Kristian Alfonso (Hope), Arleen Sorkin (Calliope), Stanley Brock (Howie), Michael Weiss (Mike), and Holly Gagnier (Ivy)—to fly in from Los Angeles to appear at her bash. The club agreed to pay for their hotel accommodations, limo service to and from the airport, and round-trip coach airfare. Diane claims she was taken advantage of by some of the stars involved, and as a result the club treasury wound up $6000 in the red. According to Diane's version of events, Stanely Brock was given tickets for an L.A.

flight to Kennedy Airport, then requested to change his destination to Newark Airport. He mysteriously showed up at Kennedy and never returned the unused tickets so that Diane could be reimbursed. She also alleges that Stanley hired a limo for ten hours so that he and his girlfriend could go sightseeing in New York, and then billed the club for the car rental. Michael Weiss also rang up a nine-and-a-half-hour limousine bill, plus $65 in cab expenses.

Days of Our Lives' *Arleen Sorkin may be a Hollywood glamour girl, but she couldn't fly first class to New Jersey.*

According to Diane, Kristian Alfonso and Arleen Sorkin put themselves in first class (adding $1235 to the Christmas luncheon tab), even though they had previously agreed to fly coach like everyone else. In a special letter to her fan club constituents, chronicling her side of the story, Diane details a battling phone conversation with Kristian's manager over the disputed plane reservations. "I said no one else is coming first class," she states. "He said, 'Well, they're not Kristian Alfonso.' . . . He told me I would never have sold all those tickets if Kristian was not coming—she was the headliner!"

After their fateful Christmas encounter in New Jersey, Kristian Alfonso and Diane Grusenski had one more unexpected run-in. It happened on July 17, 1986, at a post-awards party the evening of the Daytime Emmy ceremonies. Kristian had flown into New York to be a presenter. Diane attended the party with a friend, photographer Tony Rizzo, and Todd McKee, an actor on *Santa Barbara*. At the party, Kristian was sitting next to Brian Fronz, a top daytime programming executive at NBC. When she spotted her New Jersey nemesis, she reportedly turned to Fronz and hissed, "That's Diane Grusenski and I don't want her sitting at this table!" Diane left the party.

Later, Diane Grusenksi was banned from the NBC studio by executive producer Al Rabin. She was also informed by producer Ken Corday that the cast wanted nothing more to do with her or the club.

In all fairness to the *Days* cast members involved in this fan-club fiasco, most of their demands did seem legitimate. It's customary for daytime stars to fly first class, not coach, to all publicity events, and actors are often reimbursed for limousine and cab expenses by the promoters of such events. Moreover, keep in mind that Kristian Alfonso, Stanley Brock, and all the other performers generously volunteered their time to come from Los Angeles to New Jersey in order to help make Diane's luncheon a success.

For Diane Grusenski, though, what began as a lark ended in tears, and she obviously learned a painful lesson from her brush with the backstage aristocracy at *Days*.

Tia Carrera, a nineteen-year-old starlet who plays Jade Soong, a student nurse on *General Hospital,* got an even tougher education when she went to war with producer Gloria Monty, the grim grandam of soap opera overlords. When Tia first came on the show, she was thrown into a front-burning storyline (her character was the granddaughter of an Asian-American mobster), but when that storyline petered out, Jade soon faded into background window-dressing. Suddenly Tia was making only one ap-

ABC slapped Tia Carrera with a hefty lawsuit when she tried to leave General Hospital.

pearance a week on *GH* and earning as little as $359 for it. Though her *GH* contract (which wasn't up until August 1988) forbade her from appearing as a regular on any other series, Tia auditioned for—and won . . . a continuing, featured role on *The A-Team,* which paid her $7500 a week. She offered to do both shows simultaneously, but Gloria Monty refused. So Tia went to bankruptcy court—claiming more than $50,000 in debts— and arguing that she couldn't solve her financial problems without her *A-Team* salary. Meanwhile ABC turned around and countersued Tia and Steve Sarich, her manager/boyfriend. They were demanding $1.1 million in damages for the trouble Tia caused by breaking her contract. By the time Tia left *GH* in April 1986, the cast considered her such a prima donna that they barely bothered to speak to her. But this web eventually untangled itself. Tia was dropped by *The A-Team,* the lawsuit was dropped by ABC, and five months after storming out, Tia (as Jade) was back emptying bedpans on *General Hospital.*

A year before, *General Hospital* heartthrob Jack Wagner had tried a similar ploy and also got his wings clipped. With Tony Geary (Luke) gone and Tristan Rogers (Scorpio) getting ready to vacate Port Charles, Jack's character of rock singer Frisco Jones had emerged as the show's number-one draw. Jack also had a booming recording career on the side, so—in the middle of his three-year contract with *GH*—he demanded to re-negotiate. That kind of power play had never been tried on a soap before, and Gloria Monty was livid. She laughed in Jack's face, but that was hardly the end of it.

Without warning, Jack came down with a mysterious back ailment that forced him to miss a week's worth of shows. His publicist claimed that Jack's absence had nothing to do with contract problems. It was all just an unfortunate coincidence. According to the publicist, Jack had "hurt his back moving furniture and his doctor had ordered him to stay in bed." Gloria Monty didn't send him flowers; but neither did she waste any time. She quickly hired newcomer Kevin Bernhardt (Apollonia Kotero's real-life boyfriend) to replace him. Bernhardt did thirty-one scenes for Jack, and after Jack returned to the show, Gloria added insult to injury by creating a new major role for Bernhardt (Dr. Kevin O'Connor), which

On General Hospital *Jack Wagner shares the spotlight with (l-r) Kristina Malandro, Sam Behrens, and Jackie Zeman.*

allowed her to keep him around permanently. He and Jack were often forced to do scenes together, and occasionally the writers added gratuitous, hidden allusions in the scripts to Jack's backstage battles with the show. For example, Frisco's brother, Dr. Tony Jones, once ordered him to stop whining about being underpaid (as a police cadet).

■   ■   ■

Soap writers and producers often find unique ways of exacting revenge on actors who get out of hand. The late Irna Phillips, creator of *As the World Turns* and *Guiding Light,* was infamous for her relentless storyline guillotine. If Irna took a dislike to a particular actor or actress, their fate was sealed no matter how popular they were. In 1972 she made up her mind to kill off the character of Liz Stewart—*World Turns'* leading heroine—because Irna (a virginal Midwestern spinster) was appalled at the fact that Jane House, who played Liz, was moonlighting as a stripteaser in the Broadway hit *Lenny.* Irna thought of the leading men and ladies on her soaps almost as her exclusive, private property—she couldn't abide the idea that one of them was doing a nude scene every night before hundreds of New York theatergoers. So Irna devised swift retribution. One day Jane House glanced at her *World Turns* script and noticed there were one or two stage directions to cough; the next day she discovered she had an incurable form of pneumonia!

Ironically, Irna's plot to punish Jane House for her flagrant misconduct backfired. As Liz Stewart lay dying, loyal viewers bombarded the CBS switchboard with angry protests, threatening to stop watching *World Turns* if Liz were allowed to expire. The network stepped in and demanded a recount. They forced Irna to save her dying heroine's life, which she grudgingly agreed to do. Overnight Liz was magically cured of her incurable pneumonia (the remedy: a simple pep talk from her no-nonsense mother-in-law made Liz instantly throw off the ghost and yearn to live again!). But Jane House was so infuriated by Irna's tactics that at contract-renewal time she left the show and was replaced by a new actress, Judith McGilligan. After a few months, Irna put the kibosh on her, too. This time Liz was supposed to die in a raging fire on her wedding night. (This was characteristic of Irna's strange view of soap opera happiness: one night of bliss inexorably led to an eternity of gore, horror, and catastrophe.)

But now Irna became embroiled in a private war with Proctor & Gamble, which owned and sponsored *World Turns.* They insisted that Irna find an alternative mode of death for Liz Stewart. On *Search for Tomorrow,* another one of their shows, actress Kathryn Walker was already scheduled to go mad and immolate herself by torching the living room drapes with a lighted candelabrum.

In her accumulated rage at Procter & Gamble, *As the World Turns* producer Fred Bartholomew, Judith McGilligan, Jane House, and possibly even the author of the Broadway play *Lenny,* Irna sulkily concocted one of the silliest demises ever seen on soap opera: she had Liz trip on the hem of her negligee the morning after the wedding, fall up the stairs (not down!), hit the landing abdomen first, and die (before the next commercial break) of a ruptured spleen.

But even then Irna's wrath wasn't appeased. Along with Judith McGilligan, eight other actors were fired—nearly the entire Stewart family (Liz's husband, brother, daughter, stepdaughter, baby nurse; even her husband's ex-wife, ex-mother-in-law, and ex-wife's brand-new bridegroom). In her obsessive attempt to purge *As the World Turns* of plots and characters who'd become the bane of her scriptwriting life, Irna couldn't rest easily until she'd rid the show of every last vestige of Liz Stewart's memory.

Ironically, Irna's reign of terror was short-lived. Viewers refused to get over Liz Stewart's death and, in their grief, began turning to other soaps on other channels. In the summer of 1974, Irna Phillips—the seventy-one-year-old archangel of soap writers and the woman who'd created the very first episode of *As the World Turns*—was herself replaced by new scriptwriters, Robert Soderberg and Edith Sommer. Irna insisted that she was leaving to write her memoirs, tentatively titled *The Ivory Tower,* but those pages never saw the light of day. Six months later, during the start of the Christmas holiday season, Irna died quietly in her sleep in her Chicago apartment, apparently of natural causes. But those in the soap world who'd watched first-hand the intensity of her struggle with Procter & Gamble knew better. Dismissed from her job, cut off from soap writing—which had been her opiate and her life for so long—Irna simply had no reason to live. Like one of her own doomed serial heroines, she sighed one last time, then gave up the fight and promptly died of heartbreak.

AND BABY
MAKES
THREE

*I*n 1949 Ingrid Bergman's scandalous affair with Italian filmmaker Roberto Rossellini shocked the world. The subsequent birth of their illegitimate son, Robertino, fanned the flames and nearly destroyed the Swedish film star's Hollywood career.

Ingrid Bergman had broken moviedom's cardinal rule—don't get caught having an affair—but her situation was hardly unique. She wasn't the first actress to face the grueling ordeal of an unplanned, out-of-wedlock pregnancy, and she certainly wouldn't be the last.

Joan Collins and Kate O'Mara—*Dynasty*'s diabolical sisters—both "got into a bit of trouble," as the fan magazines used to euphemistically phrase it, early in their careers. In 1960, several years after her divorce from her first husband, British actor Maxwell Reed, Joan became pregnant while engaged to Hollywood's newest sex star, Warren Beatty. Although they were planning to get married (at some indefinite future date), Joan didn't feel ready—or willing—to tie herself down to motherhood. She chose to have an abortion.

A wise choice perhaps. As it turned out, the engagement didn't last very long. Her romance with Beatty went down the drain as quickly as many of her other love affairs (the list included Nicky Hilton, Ryan O'Neal, Sydney Chaplin, Laurence Harvey, and Cloris Leachman's husband, George Englund).

Generally, it was Joan who orchestrated each scenario from torrid beginning to tepid end, but in the case of Warren Beatty she didn't get to control the final fade-out. When Warren went off to film *Splendor in the Grass,* their relationship was doomed. During the long weeks off on location, he started carrying on with costar Natalie Wood (then married to Robert Wagner). When Joan got wind of it, she threw Warren's engagement ring back in his face. Afterward, she never regretted having ended the romance—or the pregnancy.

Kate O'Mara's story is a little more complex. Born in Leicester, England, the daughter of a Royal Air Force flyer, Kate's life has been almost as up and down as that of Caress Morell, the tainted vixen she plays on *Dynasty.* Kate married at the age of twenty-one and that union produced a son, Dickon, now twenty-three. But the couple soon went their separate ways, and to this day Kate refuses to mention her ex-husband in print or even to acknowledge him by name. "I've never told the press who he is and I never will," she stubbornly declares.

When Dickon was two years old, Kate (reportedly poverty-stricken at the time) gave birth to another son whom she later gave up for adoption. According to the birth certificate, this son—named Patrick O'Mara—was born on May 12, 1965, on the way to St. Helier Hospital in London. His mother was listed as "Kate O'Mara, an actress, of 6a Lingfield Road, Wimbledon." The father's name was left blank.

When Patrick was a few months old, he was adopted by Derek Linde, a businessman, and his wife, Joy. They changed his name to Christopher and raised him as their own son. They apparently told him nothing about his real mother until he was nearly twenty years old.

According to the *National Enquirer,* money—or rather the lack of it—was the prime motivation behind Kate's anguished decision to give up her son. "I could barely support my other child," she recently said. "I only wanted the best for my baby."

After the adoption was finalized, Kate tried to make her peace, as best she could, with what she'd done. It was impossible to forget Patrick, but she was determined to forge ahead with her life. In the ensuing years she focused all her energy on raising Dickon and establishing herself as a successful actress. Her first appearances were in low-budget British horror films like 1971's *The Vampire Lovers,* a gory Gothic tale about lesbian vampires. That same year Kate married for the second time, but she and actor-director Jeremy Young were divorced five years later.

Eventually she worked her way up to Shakespearean roles, which are still considered the highest level of accomplishment in the British theater. Kate dazzled the public in productions of *Macbeth, Antony and Cleopatra,* and *Taming of the Shrew;* and in 1980 she even starred in her own TV series, *Triangle,* a British version of *Love Boat.* But she remained pretty much unknown to American audiences until *Dynasty* producers Richard and Esther Shapiro imported her to become Alexis's new nemesis. Kate won the role after competing against sixty other British actresses.

Ironically, Kate's skyrocketing TV career also helped reunite her with Christopher Linde, the son she'd abandoned twenty years before. When Chris, who was working in the mail-order department at Harrod's in London, learned that Kate O'Mara was his natural mother, his whole world did a somersault. He was shocked at first, but then grew eager to get in touch with her. In 1985 he made his dream come true—and mother and son shared a brief, tearful reunion shortly before Kate left England to start work on *Dynasty*.

According to the *Star,* Chris located her through her theatrical agent. A meeting was arranged on neutral ground—at a house in the London suburbs. Chris wore his best suit and tie for the occasion, but was so nervous that he stopped off at a pub first for a few beers. He later told a British newspaper, "It wasn't just a shock to find out I wasn't who I thought I was—it was an even bigger shock to discover my mother was someone I watch on TV."

Their encounter was awkward, of course, and not without pain. Chris wanted to know how Kate could have blocked out the past so completely. She assured him that wasn't the case at all. Over the years she'd never forgotten him. Whenever his birthday came around, she always felt depressed, wondering where he was and what had become of him. Being separated from him had caused her "more grief than anyone could ever know."

Kate tried to explain her reason for giving him up. She talked about her financial troubles at the time when Christopher was born, and recalled how hard it was for a single woman to raise one child by herself, let alone two. She had simply wanted her little boy to have the best chance possible at a happy, well-adjusted life. She knew he'd have it growing up in a middle-class home with both a mother and a father—not with her. That's why she'd had to give him up.

Could Christopher accept that? Maybe not instantly, but some day perhaps. Undoubtedly, neither Kate nor Christopher expected to change twenty years' worth of history in a few minutes. Still, this turned out to be a very cathartic—and hopeful—encounter for both mother and son. At the end, they both broke down in tears and hugged, promising to keep in touch.

Kate O'Mara was fortunate enough to get a second chance with the child she put up for adoption. But actress Kate Mulgrew may never have that opportunity. Few adopted children are ever united with their biological parents.

In recent years Mulgrew had enjoyed a fair measure of success on the tube. She's guest-starred as Ted Danson's politician girlfriend on *Cheers,* romanced Steve Kanaly on *Dallas,* and at one point even had her own mystery series, *Kate Columbo,* a spin-off of the popular Peter Falk show. But Kate's real-life maternity story unfolded before she ever became a prime-time crime-solver—or played the saintly Mother Elizabeth Seton in the TV movie *A Time for Miracles.* It happened back in 1977 when she was still playing Mary Ryan Fenelli on the ABC daytime soap *Ryan's Hope.*

When Kate, who was single and dating an aspiring stage director, became pregnant, the show made every effort to accommodate her situation. Since her soap character, Mary, was married (to Jack Fenelli, played by Michael Levin), it was relatively easy for the show's writers to weave Kate's expectant motherhood into the storyline. Still, it was a sticky situation. All through her pregnancy, Kate maintained a high profile on the show, but became totally reclusive as far as the press was concerned. She refused to give interviews or even confirm or deny her condition (although

On Ryan's Hope *Kate Mulgrew married Michael Levin; in real life she didn't marry the father of her baby, an aspiring director.*

it was more than apparent to anyone observing her at close range). Shortly after the child was born, she gave it up for adoption.

Fearing the negative publicity that might ensue, ABC-TV begged the press not to make any mention of the birth or the adoption, and most publications complied. But in its August 1977 issue, *Daytimers Magazine* ran a short feature on the event, headlined AND BABY MAKES TWO. The article stated that "Kate Mulgrew gave birth to her child, a girl, on May 4 in Manhattan. . . . An inside source at the studio says that Kate had made arrangements to have her child adopted by a Roman Catholic couple prior to her birth, and that, as far as they know, 'the child was already on the way to its new parents.' . . . Kate had once commented that if she ever became pregnant while unwed, she would raise the child. Guess she changed her mind."

Ironically, Kate had to endure the rigors of labor twice, in a manner of speaking. Shortly after she gave birth to her own baby, her character, Mary Fenelli, gave birth to a daughter, Ryan, on-screen. The writers devoted an entire episode to Mary's labor, showing her awake and aware, faithfully following the Lamaze natural-childbirth procedure. Kate turned in a bravura performance, simulating the whole ordeal she'd just gone through, contractions and all. It must have been especially difficult, considering that Mary—unlike Kate— got to keep her baby daughter.

A while later, Kate left the New York-based *Ryan's Hope* to try her luck in Hollywood. At her farewell party on the *Ryan's Hope* set, head writer Claire Labine called Kate "one of the bravest actresses I've ever known." She didn't give any specific reason for saying that, but the meaning behind her remark seemed obvious. The real-life drama Kate Mulgrew had recently starred in was something no one in that room would ever forget.

What Kate Mulgrew and Kate O'Mara elected to do took courage—but other choices can be equally heroic, too. Early in 1973, when Sharon DeBord came down with morning sickness, cultural attitudes toward unwed mothers were starting to loosen up, but weren't quite so liberated as they are now. Up to that time, no soap opera star had ever risked public condemnation by daring to become pregnant when she wasn't wearing a wedding ring.

During the 1960s two Hollywood rebels, Vanessa Redgrave and Mia Farrow, had borne illegitimate children without suffering any of the hysterical backlash that had once greeted Ingrid Bergman. But soaps, even in the consciousness-raising 70s, were still a very conservative medium. Advertisers insisted that characters and storyliners reinforce traditional American values—the strength of the family, the sanctity of marriage. So

Sharon DeBord was putting a lot on the line—perhaps too much. Was she about to throw away a very lucrative and successful career on *General Hospital* by coming out of the closet as soap opera's first real-life unwed mother?

The backstage story that unraveled had more twists and turns than a soap opera script!

For starters, in this case conception was no accident—it was very much a planned decision. Sharon had her own reasons for getting pregnant. After two terrible divorces, she wasn't exactly enamored of the domestic life, but she knew her biological clock was ticking and she wanted a baby.

The baby's father, who'd been her boyfriend of some time, was a rock musician. He traveled a lot and was hardly a serious candidate for marriage. When she discovered that she was pregnant, Sharon told him the news, but they never really discussed settling down. From the start, they both agreed that the child would be her responsibility—and hers alone.

Other girls in her so-called bind might have been terrified, but Sharon was overjoyed. This was something she had planned and prayed for. "It was no accident that I became pregnant," she later revealed. "I've wanted a child for a long time."

Her only fear at all during those first few months was that she might miscarry. And for a time it seemed possible. Sharon was beside herself, and that's when it became obvious how desperately she wanted this child. She scrupulously followed doctor's orders, eating right and getting as much rest as possible, doing everything in her power to make sure that she wouldn't lose the baby.

As the weeks progressed and the danger of a miscarriage subsided, Sharon refused to hide her pregnancy, even though she had no idea how her producer and network might react. On *General Hospital*, Nurse Sharon Pinkham, the character she played, was a paragon of virtue. ABC wasn't sure how viewers would take the news about Sharon's forthcoming little bundle from the stork. Would they start sending her hand-knitted baby booties or angry letters demanding her dismissal?

To play it safe, ABC could have written her off the show before her waistline started to balloon. But Joe Young, producer of *General Hospital*, convinced the network muckey-mucks to hold their horses. A fair-minded man in general, he'd always had a soft spot in his heart for Sharon. In fact, he was more than just her boss—he was her mentor. He had discovered Sharon a few years back when she was appearing in a minor Los Angeles stage production. He'd been so captivated by her performance that he'd brought her on *General Hospital* as an under-fiver and gradually molded her into one of the show's most popular heroines.

Now, thanks to Joe's intervention, ABC agreed to keep the faith. Sharon could stay on the show through her eighth month of pregnancy, then she'd receive a standard two-month maternity leave. They decided to write her pregnancy into the scripts and let Nurse Sharon have a baby, too. Plotwise, that posed no difficulties for the writers, since Nurse Sharon was already happily married to Dr. Henry Pinkham.

Off-screen, Sharon enjoyed a close friendship with Peter Kilman, who played her TV husband. They got along like brother and sister, and Peter was very protective of her. Less than halfway through her pregnancy, the music man dropped out of her life, and once he was gone Peter began to assume a more prominent role in the forthcoming blessed event. When Sharon needed a date, Peter (a confirmed bachelor) would escort her to movie premieres and cast parties. He helped her shop for the nursery and made sure she got plenty of rest and exercise. On set he'd bring her pillows, surprise her with little gifts, and give her back rubs when she became uncomfortable. Off set he doted on her, too. He even helped her find a new apartment. Midway through her pregnancy Sharon told a friend that "Peter persuaded me to give up my old apartment in North Hollywood and take a cottage on the beach. He lives just around the corner from me now, and we take long walks on the beach together. He's very protective of me and he's almost as excited about the baby as I am."

Sharon's involvement with Peter would never be a romance. They weren't in love with each other—and they both accepted that. As a matter of fact, Sharon really wasn't in the market for a new relationship. With the rock musician just a memory now, she was perfectly content to be solo for a while. She fully expected to have her baby alone—and raise it alone. Besides, with her belly blossoming by leaps and bounds, what man would bother to look at her twice? Or so she thought. For that's when fate played the strangest trick of all. Somewhere between her last day of morning sickness and her first Lamaze class, Sharon fell in love.

To understand how that happened, it's necessary to leave Sharon and Los Angeles for a moment and shift the scene three thousand miles east, back to New York. There, in the early spring of 1973, a macho young actor named Antony Ponzini was starring on another ABC soap, *One Life to Live*. He played Vince Wolek, a blue-collar hothead who drank beer, strutted around in sweaty T-shirts, and lost his temper a lot. But underneath all that bowling-alley bravado, he really had a marshmallow for a heart. In fact, Vince was a lot like Tony himself.

Like most of the actors on *One Life to Live*, Tony used to hang out in the makeup room during rehearsal breaks. The hairdressers and makeup men kept a TV monitor blasting all day, and Tony would catch bits and pieces of all the ABC soaps, including *General Hospital,* which came on right after *One Life.* Eventually, like millions of other soap watchers, Tony got hooked on *Hospital,* and over a long period of time he developed a crush on one of the show's prettiest actresses—Sharon DeBord.

That's when the plot thickened.

Early in 1973 Tony took his annual two-week vacation from *One Life* and flew out to Los Angeles to catch up with friends. A year earlier he'd been head over heels in love with an actress on his own show, (they'd even rented apartments in the same Manhattan building), but now he was between girlfriends—and without a care in the world.

In L.A., the first thing Tony did was get in touch with one of his closest pals, Martin West, the redheaded actor who played Dr. Phil Brewer on *General Hospital.* Martin invited Tony to visit the set and arranged for him to meet his dream girl—Sharon DeBord. Tony wasn't surprised by her appearance (he'd already been forewarned about her pregnancy), but his reaction when they met . . . well, that was another story. Sharon's condition didn't put him off at all. He was absolutely charmed by her. He even asked her out.

They were an odd couple, to say the least, but somehow the rough New York bachelor and the laid-back California mother-to-be hit it off. "Maybe because we're both so cocky and independent," Tony once said. At any rate, it didn't take them long to discover that they cared for each other—a lot.

A few days later Tony returned to New York, but they kept up a

Sharon DeBord, Tony Ponzini, and son Lucas . . . a happy family after a few real-life soap opera twists.

long-distance romance for the rest of the pregnancy. On June 17, 1973, Sharon gave birth to a son, Lucas, and on Septembr 7 she became Mrs. Antony Ponzini.

Ironically, despite all the support and understanding that the network, the cast, and producer Joe Young had given her, Sharon was no longer interested in staying on *General Hospital*. Shortly after Lucas' birth, she decided to leave the show and the newlyweds settled in New York, where they stayed until Tony finished out his *One Life to Live* contract. Then Tony, Sharon, and little Lucas all moved back to California on a permanent basis.

Sharon had been looking forward to motherhood for a long time, so her newfound domesticity was hardly implausible. But Tony surprised everyone, including himself, by taking to instant fatherhood like a duck to water. A real change had come over him. Tony, who'd once had an eye for every pretty girl in town, wasn't looking beyond his own doorstep now. The former swinger was suddenly content to spend his weekends pushing Lucas' swing in Santa Monica Park.

■   ■   ■

Today, of course, hardly anyone raises an eyebrow when an unmarried actress goes the maternity route. Times have changed. In recent years, there's been proliferation of single celebrity moms, including Jessica Lange and Farrah Fawcett, while young stars like Amy Irving and Tatum O'Neal didn't bother to tie the knot until several months after their babies were born. Even the term "unwed mother" has become laughably out of date.

And the soap scene is catching up with the rest of the world. Nobody got nervous in 1983 when twice-divorced *Young & Restless* star Melody Thomas announced that she was going to become a mother. Melody proudly posed for photos and gladly gave interviews all through her pregnancy. She never worried about being written off the show, never wondered if her fans would desert her because of her unconventional behavior. Reporters were even invited to visit the home she shared with makeup man Carlos Yeaggy, the baby-to-be's father. After the birth of their beautiful, dark-haired, dark-eyed daughter, Alexandra, the three of them made an enviable family indeed. But Carlos and Melody's domestic bliss was short-lived—as was her single-mother status. Carlos moved out when Alexandra was barely a year old, and Melody later surprised everyone by marrying her *Young & Restless* producer Ed Scott.

But Melody's story is no longer unique. Other daytime actresses are finding a new sense of fulfillment in rocking the cradle, too, with or without husbands. Kerry Sherman, who created the role of Amy Perkins on *Santa Barbara*, recently became the soap world's newest single mother—and hardly suffered a single moment's doubt or anxiety over her decision. Even though Kerry and her boyfriend, cameraman Jack English, aren't married, Kerry's pregnancy wasn't accidental. "Like a lot of women my age," says Kerry, who's over thirty, "I had gone after a career, not a family, but then I realized that I didn't want to miss out on motherhood. And I'm glad I didn't. Kerry's father and I have been living together for four years, and we've agreed that if we should split up, our daughter Erin will remain with me. So far, marriage isn't something we've discussed. I don't really think about it."

Kerry worked on *Santa Barbara* all through her pregnancy, and shortly before Erin's arrival in 1985, the other actresses on the show organized a baby shower for her. "But the men got very upset that they were being excluded," laughs Kerry. "They said, 'This is 1985 and we want to be invited, too!' So the men all chipped in and bought a crib for the baby— then they tried to storm the celebration!" *Santa Barbara*'s head writers, Jerome and Bridget Dobson, sent Erin a pair of mink booties (with a note saying that it's never too soon for a girl to start wearing mink!) and the show's producer, Mary-Ellis Bunim, let Kerry install a crib in her dressing room so Erin could come to work with her.

"Everyone on the set adores Erin," says Kerry, "especially the single women who've never had children. Some of the actresses fight over who gets to hold her next. I can't help laughing when they come into my dressing room to play with her, and she throws up all over their cashmere sweaters. Judith McConnell (Sofia) is just great with her, though. She'll say, 'Kerry, the baby's crying. Let me take her. I know how to make her feel better.' And I'll laugh and say, 'Okay, Judith, knock yourself out!' "

Even Kerry's mom, 1940ish film star Peggy Ryan, has accepted Kerry's decision to stay single. "Jack's family and mine would have preferred us to be married," admits Kerry, "but they know this is our choice and they respect it. Actually, Judith Anderson (who plays Minx Lockridge on *Santa Barbara*) is the only one who's upset. Dame Judith calls Jack up all the time and says, 'So when are you going to propose to her, young man? I think it's high time you two got married, you know!' "

Dame Judith Anderson?!

Can this possibly be the same woman who's one of the most renowned stars of the English-speaking stage? Who, as Medea and Lady Macbeth, gave new meaning to the word blood-curdling? Turns out even if she is a WASP—and a dame to boot—she's really just a Jewish mother at heart.

DEATH
WISH

In the world of soap opera, death has many faces. On-screen, characters are frequently killed off for the sake of a dramatic cliff-hanger. They blow up in cars, burn up in fires, crash their planes, drown, suffocate, topple off cliffs, succumb to poison, catch an assassin's bullet, or fall prey to some never quite defined, but palpably fatal disease. In nearly twenty years of *One Life to Live*, Michael Storm, who plays Dr. Larry Wolek, has been to more funerals than he can remember. "We've buried half the town of Llanview," he laughs, "but the population keeps growing anyway. That's because half the people we bury don't stay dead. The same actors keep turning up as the long-lost twin brothers of the characters they used to play."

Soap audiences thrive on the maudlin and the macabre. There are tales of viewers who actually dress up in black when their favorite TV characters kick the bucket. They sit grief-stricken in front of their television sets, just as if they were witnessing the funeral of a beloved friend or family member.

Sometimes contract negotiations intervene, and a hero has to bite the bullet because the star behind the soap-opera mask won't re-sign on the dotted line. When a popular actor makes up his mind to leave the show, the producers often choose to guillotine his character, figuring it's a waste of time to recast. If an actor is closely identified with his TV role, it's hard to get viewers to accept a replacement. Termination—or sending the character on a permanent vacation—become the only story options. The death of *Dallas'* Bobby Ewing was a perfect example of that kind of backstage situation—so was the final fadeout of *Knots Landing's* Sid Fairgate. In both cases the actors who played the roles (Patrick Duffy and Don Murray) refused to sign new contracts. But it's interesting to note that the minute Duffy agreed to return to *Dallas,* his character had no trouble rising from the dead. In plotline purgatory, where there's a will there's a way. In Bobby's case, it turned out that his wife Pam had merely dreamed the entire season he was absent from the show. Other characters come back to life because corpses were never found or identified properly—or, in the case of *Dallas'* Mark Graison, because he was off somewhere having a secret remission to that supposedly fatal blood disease. On soap opera, the miracle of resurrection is a never-ending occurrence.

The scriptwriters deal very glibly with life and death, which makes for high ratings and happy viewers, but for an extremely tense group of stars. Soap opera acting isn't the most secure profession in the world. "On Monday's show my character had a slight headache," recalls one actress, "and by Friday I was dying of a brain tumor." In the 1970s actress Jill Harmon was hired to play a character named Maria Marino on *As the World Turns.* Two other actors were brought on to play her husband and brother. It certainly looked as if she was going to be part of an important new family on the show, but then the writers suddenly changed their minds. One day, while studying her script, Jill noticed something peculiar: in the last scene of that episode her character underwent emergency gall-bladder surgery. It was, in fact, the last *As the World Turns* script that Jill ever saw. Her character died on the operating table.

Getting fired without warning is a way of life on soaps, but demoralizing nonetheless. "It's a kind of death," contends one daytimer, who's found herself written off two different soaps without notice. "When you see your storyline start to wind down, and you first begin to wonder if they want to get rid of you, you react in much the same way that a person with a terminal illness does. You go through all the same phases—denial, anger, depression, and finally acceptance. The first month I wasn't used on the show, I kept telling myself, 'Don't worry, it's all right. Your story-line's bound to heat up again soon—next week they'll probably use you in all five shows.' Well, that didn't happen, and the second month I got so angry I wanted to beat down the producer's door and tell her, 'How dare you treat me like this?' The third month I just gave up and became a recluse. I didn't even want to leave the house. By the fourth month, I finally accepted the fact that I was losing my job—that my contract wouldn't be renewed—and began to put my life in order. I got a new résumé together, called my agent, and started making the casting rounds."

Louise Sorel found herself in that kind of bind on the NBC soap *Santa Barbara,* but she did manage to turn the tables in her favor. When the writers refused to create an interesting storyline for her character, Augusta Lockridge, she quickly negotiated another role on a different soap. In fact, her transition was so swift that while her last *Santa Barbara* scenes were still airing, Louise was already playing an elegant attorney named Judith Sanders on *One Life to Live*. But even though Louise got the last laugh, there was a great deal of pain involved. "Actors are very protective of their territory," she notes. "Sometimes I'll tune in *Santa Barbara* to watch some of my friends, but it's a depressing experience. I get so angry seeing another actress sitting in the Lockridge living room, I feel like it's my house, my furniture—and the other actress is an intruder. It's like seeing your ex-husband with his new wife! Sometimes I'll start crying and think, 'Why did I have to leave it all?' "

Some stars never really bounce back. An actor on *Guiding Light* was so devastated after losing his role that he never worked again. He had no confidence in himself anymore. Every time he had to face an audition, he'd develop some kind of vague illness that forced him to cancel. *Dynasty*'s Al Corley hasn't been heard from very much on the TV scene since parting company with his role of Steve Carrington, and Pamela Sue Martin—the show's original Fallon—has never done another series. Audrey Peters was the star of *Love of Life* for more than two decades, but since the show's demise, she's only done minor, one- and two-day roles on other soaps.

Some actors seem to come equipped with a built-in death wish. It's almost as if they truly wanted to fail. Or else the pressure of working on a successful show is so grueling that they cave in. An actress who was in her early twenties was found comatose in her dressing room on a CBS soap, the victim of a drug overdose. She was rescued and rushed to the hospital just in time, and later replaced on the air by another actress while she entered an intensive rehabilitation program. But she isn't the only soap performer who's come close to the edge. Few, though, are willing to talk about it.

One actor who isn't afraid to share his feelings is Guy Mack, who plays Dr. Patrick O'Connor on *General Hospital*. Back in college, Patrick originally set out to be a professional trumpet player, but a severe accident permanently damaged his lip and forced him to give up the trumpet. Unable to deal with it, he went into a depression and for a time came close to suicide. "I was devastated," he recalls. "Music was all I'd known for years. My number-one recourse was suicide. I almost did it a few times, but somebdy was always there to save me. I guess it just wasn't my time to go."

Another daytimer-with-a-death-wish, Brenda Benet, wasn't quite so lucky. On April 7, 1982, the *Days of Our Lives* star was found dead in the guest bathroom of her Los Angeles home. When the police broke down the bathroom door, they found her lying on the rug, clutching a .38 caliber gun. The coroner's report later revealed that she had killed herself by shooting a bullet through her open mouth. The bullet had ricocheted off a tooth and gone right through her head.

The world at large was shocked, but friends and castmates were hardly surprised. The thirty-seven-year-old actress, one of the most tormented souls ever to grace a soap, had been emotionally unstable for some time. Her despondency had grown even worse since the death of her six-year-old son, Christopher, just thirteen months before. Taking her life was merely the final step of a long, dark journey. By April 1982, when Brenda died, her life had become unbearable. As she saw it, death was the only way out, the only chance off the merry-go-round.

When Brenda first came to Hollywood, nobody could have predicted such a tragic end for her. Beautiful and talented, she seemed destined for stardom, and Hollywood's most eligible bachelors flocked around her. In short order, she married TV actor Paul Peterson, who had starred on *The Donna Reed Show,* but later divorced him and wed another actor, Bill Bixby. While Bill scored major successes with *The Courtship of Eddie's Father* and *The Incredible Hulk,* Brenda seemed content to stay on the

In the late 1970s a new storyline brought Brenda Benet and Bill Hayes to-gether on Days of Our Lives. *(Natasha Ryan played his daughter.)*

sidelines and let her career slide. She was particularly devoted to their young son, Christopher, and wasn't anxious to leave him. But when her seven-year marriage to Bixby fell by the wayside in the summer of 1979, Brenda accepted the role of Lee Carmichael on *Days of Our Lives.*

Nevertheless, Christopher remained her first priority. "Being a mother is the most challenging thing I've ever done," she said. "Christopher's so bright and sensitive—he's the joy of my life. I've never known anyone like him."

The contrast between Brenda, the off-screen devoted mother and on-screen dragon lady was startling indeed. Sometimes, it seemed, Brenda herself had a hard time deciding who she really was. From the moment she made her first entrance on *Days of Our Lives,* fans were enthralled with her villainous TV character, who was both carnal and conniving, and a little of Lee Carmichael began to rub off on Brenda. Backstage, according to reports, Brenda began to play out a very parallel script. She fought bitterly with one castmate and had an adulterous affair with another. She earned a reputation for being high-strung and temperamental, although no one ever questioned her talent. Brenda dominated every scene she was in.

Meanwhile, her private life was becoming a real soap opera, too. Her bitter divorce from Bill Bixby made banner headlines. Brenda petitioned the court to put a restraining order on her soon-to-be ex-husband, preventing him from claiming any of their community property. She claimed he wanted to remove furniture from their luxurious home in the Mandeville Canyon section of Los Angeles. Since the separation, Bixby was dividing his time between his plush one-bedroom apartment at Universal Studios, where he filmed *The Incredible Hulk,* and a fully furnished yacht which he kept anchored at a nearby marina. According to Brenda, he was living as well, if not better, than she and Christopher were, and had no need to take any of the furniture in the Mandeville Canyon house. She told the court, "He is an extremely well paid entertainer who could well afford to rent furniture."

Despite their well-published disputes, both parents were united on one thing—their love for their son. Brenda was granted custody of the boy, but Bill remained close to him, too. Bill was adamant about one thing—that his son not be allowed to watch any episodes of *The Incredible Hulk.* He worried that if Christopher saw him transform every week from mild-mannered David Bruce Banner into his Hulk persona—a gargantuan, ugly, green monster—it might give him nightmares.

However, a much more devastating scenario lay in store than anyone could have foreseen. The most unexpected nightmare of all occurred in

March 1981 when Brenda decided to take Christopher on a harmless camping trip in the Sierra Mountains. While on the trip. Christopher, who was suffering from a cold, developed respiratory problems and had to be rushed to a hospital. The nearest one was several miles away. By the time Christopher arrived there, his breathing had become so labored that doctors had to perform an emergency tracheotomy. Often, this is an uncomplicated procedure, but during the operation Christopher went into cardiac arrest and died.

Afterward Brenda was numbed. Outwardly, she refused to let herself grieve, but inwardly she was tortured by the loss of the one human being she loved most in the world. She tried to lose herself in work, and later in a passionate love affair, but neither could give her the inner peace she so desperately needed. After Christopher's death, Brenda returned to *Days of Our Lives* very quickly—too quickly perhaps—and tried to go on as if nothing had happened. On the surface, she seemed so calm and accepting. She stunned everyone by giving interviews to the press, and whenever Brenda met with reporters, she was eager to speak about her son. She'd go on at length about Christopher's passing and about how grateful she was for all the letters of support and encouragement she had received.

For a time, Brenda seemed to become almost manic. She embarked on at least one unfortunate romance (with a black soap star) and may have been involved in other casual relationships, too. March 1982 was a particularly horrible time for her—the first anniversary of Christopher's death. It hit her very hard, and friends later conjectured that this was the turning point for her on the road to self-destruction. She now went into an even deeper depression that directly led to her suicide a month later. Her behavior near the end was very strange—almost frighteningly calm. The last week of her life Brenda made plans with two castmates to attend a party (which, of course, she never attended) and just a few days before her death, she phoned one of her favorite fan magazine editors to thank her profusely for a recent article. In retrospect, the call was obviously a farewell gesture.

According to the police report, on the day of her death Brenda had a violent argument with a lover, then began drinking about noon and ultimately decided to kill herself. She carried out her final act, lying down on a soft rug in the bathroom with a lighted candle beside her. The thirty-eight had been in her possession for some time. She had bought it for protection after receiving threatening notes from angry fans who were upset that her TV character, Lee Carmichael, had broken up the marriage of Doug and Julie Williams, the show's number-one couple.

Brenda's death sent shock waves through the *Days of Our Lives* cast. Lanna Saunders, who played Marie Horton, and her husband, actor Larry

Pressman, held a memorial service at their home for the actress' friends and colleagues, who came to share their grief, their disbelief and, most of all, their memories of Brenda. One castmate, who seemed to speak for everyone, noted, "If there really is a hereafter, at least Brenda and Christopher are together now—that's all she really wanted."

THE CASUALTIES OF *GENERAL HOSPITAL*

*G*eneral Hospital's Tony Geary's relationships with women have always been on the transient side. For a long time his star traveling companion was Kathy Kotarakis, the hair stylist on *General Hospital,* but there was definitely more friendship than fire in that relationship. He was also linked with *GH* director Marlena Laird, an occasional dinner companion, but again there was no substance to the romance. As for Tony's off-screen relationship with his TV bride, Genie Francis, there wasn't even anything to wonder about. "They're more like father and daughter off set," confided one of Tony's closest pals. "He's thirty-four, she's only eighteen. She grew up watching *Marcus Welby* and *All in the Family.* He acted on those shows, for God's sake."

Actually, Tony was much more concerned with breaking out of his Luke Spencer soap opera image—and becoming an American Elton John—than he was about settling down with the right woman, or any woman. He didn't want to be known just as a daytime Romeo. He decided to try the nightclub circuit and developed one of the raunchiest cabaret acts in memory. It was part cheap, part Chippendale's, and pure camp, with Tony bumping and grinding like a Forty-second Street stripper on stage as he belted out "Teen Angel" and "Tell Laura I Love Her."

When Tony debuted his act at Atlantic City's Playboy Hotel—with two female backup dancers called the Smut Queens—critics marveled at the crudity and sheer variety of the vulgar gestures that he managed to get away with. "His hips and pelvis worked a lot harder than his vocal cords," cracked one reviewer.

Elizabeth Taylor guested on General Hospital *as spider widow Helena Cassidine. Tony Geary nearly flubbed his lines when he met her.*

Tony was through playing the joker. Nobody was going to control his life or his career—including *General Hospital,* the show that had made him famous—and maybe that's what his outrageous nightclub act was all about. Tony was tired of playing daytime Superman, so he pranced on stage in purple tap shoes and made lewd remarks to the screaming women in the audience who'd trekked fifty or a hundred miles by bus to Atlantic City just to see him. They thought they were getting Prince Valiant—instead they got Peter Allen. But Tony didn't care. By 1982 he was getting ready to check out of *General Hospital,* and on the eve of his wildly self-stroking Atlantic City debut, he bragged that "I'm sick of being acceptable to ABC or any other network!"

Genie Francis had left the show in December 1981 (she went on to do her own prime-time soap, *Bare Essence,* and later the ABC miniseries *North and South*). At that point burnout was starting to set in and Tony was ready to quit, too. But Gloria Monty had begged him to stay one more year. Once Tony extended his contract, the problem was finding a new leading lady for him. Janine Turner—a blond, Genie Francis look-

Left: *Tony Geary fighting it out with Peter Harrel on* General Hospital, *just as he later fought it out with the show itself.* Right: *After leaving* General Hospital, *Genie Francis starred on the blockbuster miniseries* North and South.

alike—was brought in, and viewers raised holy hell. Next, ABC tried a gravel-voiced brunette—actress Demi Moore, who played reporter Jackie Templeton. But that didn't work either. Her chemistry with Tony Geary was nothing at all like the fireworks she'd later create on-screen when she teamed with Rob Lowe in *St. Elmo's Fire* and *About Last Night.*

Meanwhile ABC was getting frantic—and *General Hospital's* ratings were suddenly starting to dip. Finding the right screen partner for Tony Geary was like searching for the right foot for the magic glass slipper. There were lots of talented, good-looking actresses out there—unfortunately, none of them happened to be Cinderella. But finally she appeared— in the form of a twenty-one-year-old British beauty named Emma Samms— and the moment she teamed with Tony Geary, *General Hospital's* ratings shot right back up.

Incredibly, with her dark hair, exquisite eyes, and round gamine face, Emma Samms bore an uncanny resemblance to a young Elizabeth Taylor. Her reserved English manner, contrasted with her sensuous, come-hither smile, only added to the illusion. Emma could have easily played the society girl in *A Place in the Sun* or the well-mannered prostitute in *Butterfield 8*.

Emma joined *General Hospital* in the summer of 1982 as Holly Sutton, a kindhearted con artist who was the perfect match for ex-hustler and renegade Luke Spencer. As her TV romance with Tony Geary heated up, the press tried to read between the lines—again without success. Not that the diminutive British import was something of a wallflower. Far from it. Before bowing out of *GH* in 1985 (to join *The Colbys*) Emma would be linked hot and heavily with composer Marvin Hamlisch, *General Hospital* costar Tristan Rogers, Jon-Erik Hexum, a Chicago millionaire named Ted Field, and a prominent Los Angeles physician, who remained nameless. Tony, however, somehow never made the list.

"It's garbage! It's nonsense!" was how Tony reacted to those first tabloid headlines inferring that he and Emma were backstage soulmates and pillow partners. "I think Emma's a doll to work with. She's bright and bubbly and very professional, but we're not dating," he insisted.

Emma, who was still pretty new at the gossip game, said, "Tony and I giggle a lot on the set, but that's as far as it goes. In fact, one of the things I like best about Tony is his sense of humor. It's one of the qualities I admire most in a man." (Emma confided to a magazine that her ideal fantasy lover would actually be David Letterman.) But despite her attraction to comedy, some of her romances have taken a very serious turn indeed.

Early in 1984 Emma guest starred on *Hotel* and fell head over heels for her leading man, Jon-Erik Hexum. Emma had seen him on TV, smoldering up the screen with Joan Collins in the movie *Making of a Male Model,* and she'd been hooked ever since. "I remember watching him in that movie and thinking he was the most gorgeous man I'd ever seen," Emma recalls. "I dreamed of meeting him." She finally did when they played a modern-day Cinderella and Prince Charming on *Hotel.*

In the script, they fell madly in love and ran off together. In real life, they were soon labeled as an item and, according to one report, Emma even broke off with previous boyfriend Marvin Hamlisch to be with Hexum. But the attraction, mainly physical, didn't last. By the time of the bizarre gunshot accident that took his life on the set of his new show, *Cover Up,* Emma and Jon-Erik had cooled down considerably. Still, she was devastated by news of his death and found it difficult to get through her scenes on *General Hospital* that day. In fact, she was depressed for a long time afterward.

In 1983 Tony Geary left *General Hospital,* and Emma got a new leading man, Tristan Rogers, the Australian actor who'd been playing

Luke's sidekick, Robert Scorpio, for two years. Surprisingly enough, fans liked the Emma/Tristan matchup even better than the Emma/Tony mix and quickly gave their blessing to Holly and Robert's on-camera coupling. In poll after poll of fan-magazine readers, Emma and Tristan were anointed as the new royal lovers of soap opera.

Backstage, there was an intensity about their relationship, too—a playfulness that Tony Geary and Emma had never shared. To all appearances they couldn't have been more of an odd couple: Tristan was the resident joker; Emma's pert little nose stayed high in the air. But opposites—especially when they're both lonely—can certainly attract. It was no secret that Tristan was very unhappily married; for her part, Emma's string of dead-end romances had left her feeling empty and unfulfilled. Soon their mutual need for a little comic relief in their lives drew them together.

It all started innocently enough. During rehearsal, they constantly needled each other. Tristan would call her a "bloody Limey"; Emma would tease him back about his garbled, low-class Australian accent. Pretty soon the tricks started getting out of hand. During a scene that took place in a sauna (after Holly and Scorpio were married), the script called for Tristan to playfully try to pull Emma's towel off. "We had to cut and retape because Tristan really did pull my towel off—and all I had on was my bikini underwear!" Emma recollects.

The overtures weren't all one-sided. In return, she would buy him little gag gifts and leave funny greeting cards under his dressing room door—for no particular occasion at all.

It was inevitable that the playfulness would lead to passion. After seven stormy years together, Tristan and his wife, Barbara, were on the brink of a full-scale explosion. They'd tried breaking up several times, and tried reconciling, too. In their case, nothing seemed to work—perhaps because Tristan wasn't really ready yet to cut the emotional cords. Whatever their problems, Barbara had stood by him—and supported him—all through his years as a struggling, unsuccessful rock musician (in London) and then actor (in America). When he'd finally made it big on *General Hospital,* she had found new ways to become indispensable to him by directing his career, managing his fan club, and scheduling all his personal appearances. Strange little threads of dependency held them together. It was all they had left.

The scenario on the home front was always the same: they'd fight, Tristan would leave, then after a few hours (or sometimes a few days) he'd return. On one occasion, when reporters caught wind of the fact that

Emma Samms, with a drawing of General Hospital *given to her when she left the show, signed by cast members.*

Tristan had actually moved out and was living in his dressing room at *General Hospital,* Barbara tried to downplay the separation by telling the press that they weren't squabbling at all. They were merely having all their bathrooms renovated. Tristan was sleeping at the studio, she insisted, because it was the only place where he could shave and shower. What she couldn't explain, however, was why they hadn't rented a hotel room instead—where Barbara could have been with him (and enjoyed the use of hot-and-cold-running plumbing, too).

Finally, somebody had to leave—and, ironically, it turned out not to be Tristan, but Barbara. She packed up and moved back to Australia, while Tristan—whose health had deteriorated during their months and months of constant battling—stayed on in L.A. and began focusing on getting his life back in shape.

While Tristan was going through this turmoil, Emma was trying to get off her own emotional merry-go-round. She seemed to be moving from one attempt at a relationship to the next. They were both lonely, both in need of a little understanding and comfort, and their work situation became an added aphrodisiac. On *General Hospital* they were constantly thrown together in the most luxurious love scenes imaginable. (Holly and Robert's favorite sports were all based on body contact. They were always working up a sweat in a steambath or splashing around in a hot tub.) Doing those scenes kept Emma and Tristan at a feverish pitch all day. They were soon inseparable off the set.

Ironically, the romance lasted only as long as their professional link did. In the middle of 1985 Emma left *General Hospital* to take over the role of Fallon Carrington first on *Dynasty,* then on *The Colbys.* At the end of the year, Tristan gave notice, too. He wasn't moving on to anything specific; after four years he was just restless for change. (Tristan did return once, though, for a limited run. In September 1986, when the show was about to undergo some cast and production upheavals, Tristan agreed to reprise his Robert Scorpio role for thirteen weeks to help bolster the ratings.)

In retrospect, Emma had no bitterness about the romance. "We were friends for the longest time before we got involved," she told *Soap Opera Digest.* "We helped each other through traumatic times. . . . When we broke up there were never any cruel words. It was not an ugly situation. We started as friends and I think we always will be."

For Emma, though, the traumatic times were far from over, and she probably could have used Tristan's strong, calming presence on the set when she went off to stake her claim to *Dynasty.* Her reception there couldn't have been icier. In order to play Fallon, Emma had to affect an American accent. It gave her trouble right from the start, even though she'd already done the same thing playing an American girl in the seven-hour CBS miniseries, *Ellis Island.*

Emma had barely started on *Dynasty* when the press suddenly turned on her. *The Hollywood Reporter,* the backstage Bible of the television world, ridiculed her performance as Fallon. Other papers began hinting that *Dynasty* was secretly negotiating with Pamela Sue Martin, the original Fallon, to come back to the role.

All in all, it wasn't the best of times for her. While Emma was being crucified in print, she was also suffering from exhaustion trying to do two shows at once. Because of contractual difficulties, her exit from *General Hospital* wound up overlapping with her entrance on *Dynasty*—and all through the summer of 1985 Emma had to shuttle back and forth between both studios.

On top of that, while horseback riding in one of her first *Dynasty* scenes, Emma was thrown from the horse and took a wild spill. As she fell, she landed on the battery pack of her body microphone (which had been strapped to her back), and had to be carried off on a stretcher. One of her vertebrae was jabbing into her spine, damaging her spinal column and rupturing a disc. There was also extensive nerve damage to the lower half of her body. Her reflexes in her knees and ankles were affected, and urinary and bowel problems developed. "It was tremendously painful," Emma recalls. "Nothing from the waist down functioned properly. And my work situation became a nightmare. *Dynasty* had to reschedule every-thing because I couldn't work for almost a month. It put a real strain on *General Hospital,* too, but Gloria Monty was an angel. She rewrote the storyline so that I could do my scenes sitting up in bed and she had a dressing room installed for me right on stage, with a portable potty. That way I didn't have to walk any stairs at the studio."

But poor timing only exacerbated Emma's woes. The accident hap-pened just when she needed her strength most. She was literally fighting for her life on *Dynasty.* All through her convalescence, reports continued to circulate that she was about to be replaced as Fallon, even though Emma had been privately assured by ABC not to worry. Finally, as a public declaration of the show's faith in her, producer Esther Shapiro did something totally unexpected: she criticized *Dallas* for not sticking with Donna Reed after bringing her on as the new Miss Ellie. The message was subtle but clear to anyone who cared to read between the lines: For the moment at least, Emma's job was safe. *Dynasty* intended to stick with

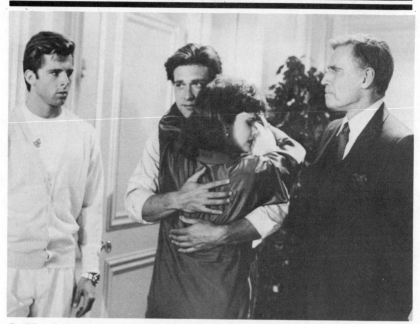

On The Colbys *Emma is torn between her love for John James and Maxwell Caulfield (left). Charlton Heston plays her father-in-law.*

her, hoping that viewers would gradually accept her, the way they'd slowly warmed up to Jack Coleman as the new Steven Carrington.

In November 1985 the network reaffirmed its faith in an even stronger way. Emma and her *Dynasty* leading man, John James, were launched into their own multimillion-dollar spin-off, *The Colbys*. To help it survive, the Shapiros gathered the most glittering collection of stars ever assembled in a prime-time cast. Even though Katharine Hepburn and Burt Lancaster quietly turned down roles, Charlton Heston, Barbara Stanwyck, Katharine Ross, and Ricardo Montalban were all eager to sign on.

Emma's daytime experience in no way prepared her for the daily setside cataclysms that occurred on *The Colbys*. During the first week of production, two million dollars' worth of furnishings and scenery were torn apart because one of the show's executives decided the sets looked tacky and uninspiring. Then Joan Collins, who played Emma Samms' mother, refused to guest star on the new series when she became convinced that it would steal ratings from her own show. Backstage, Charlton Heston bellowed, Katharine Ross raged, and Barbara Stanwyck turned cameramen and extras to ice with a single, tight-lipped call for silence on the set.

Stanwyck was bitterly unhappy from day one. She regularly fought with the producers over her scripts and publicly criticized several of the show's young stars for not knowing their lines and showing up late for rehearsals. She stormed off permanently at the end of the first season. By then *The Colbys* had slipped to subbasement position in the ratings, and next season—when it was scheduled to air opposite NBC's *Cheers* and *Night Court* and CBS's *Knots Landing*—it seemed assured of getting clobbered even worse.

Ironically, the only bright spot on Emma Samms' horizon now was her personal life. During *The Colbys'* first season, she became engaged to a Los Angeles caterer named David Corwin and they were married in London a year later during the show's Christmas break. "I've finally found the man I want to spend the rest of my life with," Emma solemnly declared. "David and I were friends for a long time before we realized we had romantic feelings for each other, so we're not really rushing into anything. I think it's best when it happens this way, when people fall in love slowly."

Emma has often mentioned that she'd like to have a large family— four children at least—and if *The Colbys* doesn't survive, it might be an opportune time for a maternity break. Despite all her trials and tribulations on *The Colbys*, though, Emma has no regrets about giving up her daytime crown. The prime-time exposure's been wonderful and because she plays John Forsythe's daughter, there's always a place waiting for her at the Carrington dinner table on *Dynasty*.

Not all soap opera queens, however, are quite that career hungry. Older stars especially know that nighttime TV's a feast or famine situation and they'd rather play it safe and stay on daytime. Emma's former castmate, septuagenarian Anna Lee, faithfully watches *MacGyver*, *Knots Landing*, and *The Colbys*, just to keep up with *General Hospital* graduates like Richard Anderson, Doug Sheehan, and, of course, Emma, but has no wish to take the prime-time plunge herself.

"I'm like Grizabella, the glamour cat," she sighs contentedly. "I've had my day in the sun. Now I'll be glad to stay on *General Hospital* for the rest of my life." The sprightly, silver-haired actress—who's a little bit younger than Kate Hepburn and a lot older than Brooke Shields—has been making movies since 1936. She's seen it all—and survived it all— and Hollywood holds no surprises for her.

Her encounter with Fritz Lang, who directed her in the 1943 war thriller *Hangmen Also Die*, gave her a real education in Hollywood sadism—and she came away with the scars to prove it. "Fritz disliked me on sight," she recalls bitterly. "He wanted one of his girlfriends to get the part, but the studio gave it to me, so he went out of his way to make things very uncomfortable for me. I knew I was in trouble the minute I walked on the set."

The real test came when Anna had to give a "smash" performance. There was a brief scene where the script called for her to push her hand through a glass window. Lang demanded that the window be made of real glass; and he refused to shoot the scene from any angle except as a close-up with Anna's full face showing. That way a stuntwoman couldn't stand in for her. He kept carrying on about realism—and Anna was too young (and too scared) to contradict him. When the cameras started rolling, she gritted her teeth and prayed that she could simply get through it in a single take.

At first it seemed like luck might be with her. When Lang yelled, "Action!," she smashed her fist through the glass so swiftly that there wasn't even a drop of blood. She came away with barely a scratch. But Lang wasn't satisfied—a few technical details weren't right, he shouted— and he demanded another take. The propmen swept up the shattered glass and a new window was quickly installed. Anna paled, but refused to show the slightest sign of fear in front of her tormentor. As cool as ever, she walked back on the set and went through all the motions again. But this time she wasn't so fortunate. When her hand went sailing through the glass, she came out with a gash severe enough to require stitches. "Today, forty-three years later, I still have a nasty scar on my wrist—a memento from Fritz Lang," she says tersely.

In 1959 another tyrannical director nearly did her in while Anna was making a film called *The Crimson Kimono* with Glenn Corbett and James Shigeta. It was a low-budget murder mystery and Anna was cast as a hippie painter. One scene required her to smoke a cigar while getting drunk. Anna, who never touched tobacco and wasn't much of a drinker, nearly wound up in the hospital.

"We kept doing take after take," she recalls, "and pretty soon the floor started weaving under me. I wound up smoking thirteen cigars and drinking an entire bottle of straight whiskey. The cameramen actually had a pool going—they were taking bets on how long it would take me to pass out. Well, somehow I didn't cave in—at least not on the set. The director got all the realistic touches he wanted, and I just kept smiling like a demented statue till we finally finished that awful scene."

Then—like a queen who won't faint until the castle's been saved and all the invaders have drowned in the moat—Anna allowed herself to savor the last laugh. "All that nauseating realism didn't help his shooting schedule

Chris Robinson and Barbara Stanger faced the press in this scene from the movie Savannah Smiles. *In real life, Chris' headline-making escapades have occasionally haunted him.*

in the long run," she chuckles. "When I got home, I was so violently ill that I took right to bed and didn't get up for three days!"

General Hospital's Chris Robinson has had similar bad luck. He's been in jail—twice. On *General Hospital* Chris plays upstanding Dr. Rick Webber, the pillar of the Port Charles community. Off-screen he seems to slide from one dark tunnel to the next. In July 1980 Chris was arrested for allegedly assaulting his estranged wife. In 1985 he was sentenced to four months in a Los Angeles minimum-security prison for income tax evasion to the tune of over $350,000.

Nothing on *General Hospital* equals the drama of Chris's own life. He was raised in a trailer park in Wilton Manors, Florida, cared for mainly by his grandparents. He acknowledges the positive influence they exerted over him, despite the fact that they fought constantly and showed him little affection. Chris's own parents were divorced. His mother worked at a nearby naval station and spent her evenings dating pilots and naval officers. She had little time for her son.

When Chris was seven, his mother decided to head for California. She took him along, but the change of scenery hardly improved their relationship. Without his grandparents' influence, Chris was left almost entirely on his own. His mother got a job as a buyer at a department store, which put food on the table and paid the rent on their tiny one-room apartment. But that was all. She squandered most of what she earned and Chris rarely had spending money. His mother's male friends were always staying over—a situation that humiliated and angered him. "When this sailor or that soldier would come for the weekend, I had to sleep on a cot on the porch," remembers Chris. "My mother spent her money on those soldiers and sailors. She never bought me a gift."

For a time, Chris went to Lynchburg, Virginia, to live with his father and stepmother. The situation there was even more appalling. His father's drinking made life a nightmare for everyone around him. Chris was ill-fed, beaten, and dressed in rags. "I lived with my alcoholic father and stepmother for about five months," he recalls. "They made me stand in a metal washtub to take a bath, where they made fun of my nudity and made me drink beer." (As a result, Chris became a lifelong teetotaler.)

After that, Chris was shunted back and forth from his grandparents in Florida to his mother in Los Angeles. During his student days at Hollywood High, he washed dishes and pumped gas to earn extra cash. At seventeen he walked out on his mother permanently when she tried to confiscate the money he'd saved to buy a car. By the time Chris had enrolled at Los Angeles City College (as a theater arts major), his mother (who was living in nearby Newport) had gone off the deep end. "She began to wear a white sheet and carried a Bible and talked about God and Com-munists," says Chris. His grandparents finally had her institutionalized after she made her way to Atlanta and was arrested on a golf course for trying to see President Eisenhower.

After graduating summa cum laude from college, Chris worked in films like *Beast of the Haunted Cave* and *Diary of a High School Bride*. Then in 1965 came a leading role in the ABC-TV series *Twelve O'Clock High*. Professionally, his star was rising, but his personal life was hardly on a smooth track. According to writer Jerry Buck, in 1961 Chris fathered an illegitimate child. Six years later he lost a paternity suit and began paying $900 a month in child support. In the mid 1960s he married Phyllis Yarwood, left Hollywood for nine years, and moved back to Florida so they could raise their young son, Christopher, Jr., in a smog-free environment.

By 1978 Chris was back in L.A. with a new wife, realtor Sandy Tennant, and a new job, playing Rick Webber on *General Hospital*. But, by his own admission, he remained almost umbilically tied to his ex-wife,

Phyllis. Even after the divorce, there had been several attempts to reconcile, and his courtship with Sandy became an emotional battlefield. "I totally walked away from Sandy—more than once," Chris confides. "I'd say, 'Sandy, I've got to try to make that marriage work.' And she'd say, 'I know. I love you. And I will always love you. But you know what you have to do.' I even spent one summer driving my ex-wife and my son all over the country."

In 1980 Chris walked away from Sandy for good, but this time Phyllis Yarwood had nothing to do with it. There was a new woman in his life—a twenty-year-old stage technician named Rhonda Plasterer. On July 9, 1980, things reached a fevered pitch. During his *General Hospital* lunch break, Chris went to the Beverly Hills house where he'd lived with Sandy and tried to remove his personal belongings. He brought along Rhonda and a team of Mexican moving men. Sandy wasn't home when Chris pulled up, but she arrived shortly afterward. An argument ensued—and all hell broke loose.

Sandy alleged that Chris "started breaking up furniture" and tried to leave with valuable Indian artifacts that they'd collected together during their marriage. According to Sandy, "When I ran out to the moving truck to try to stop him, one of the Indian pots accidentally broke—and Chris knocked me down. Meanwhile Rhonda got behind the wheel of the truck to drive away. Not thinking straight, I stood in front of the truck to try to stop her, but Rhonda kept driving and knocked me over." Sandy was later taken to UCLA Medical Center for treatment. Chris and Rhonda spent four hours in jail until their release was secured by ABC attorneys.

According to Chris, Sandy was hardly an innocent bystander. He'd notified her that he had court permission to come by and pick up his belongings, and she'd raised no objection. He also denied that he started smashing up furniture and artifacts in a fit of temper. "Why would I destroy my own property? It doesn't make sense," he said. Furthermore, he claimed that Sandy tried to make it impossible for him to leave. "She drove up and blockaded my moving truck," Chris told the press. "Her teenage daughter drove up the other way and blocked us, too, and the maid drove a third car in." As Chris described it, Sandy got into a scuffle with the Mexicans, began smashing $10,000 worth of pots and started hitting Rhonda (who happened to be recovering from surgery). Chris's only intention was to restrain his estranged wife, not harm her. "I have eighteen unbiased witnesses to substantiate the facts," Chris stated at the time. As further proof he noted that all charges had been quickly dropped. A friend of Sandy's—a woman named Pearl—had been at the scene and had made

Chris Robinson and his last wife, Rhonda Plasterer, met on the set of General Hospital.

the original citizen's arrest. She never showed up in court to pursue her allegations against Chris or Rhonda.

Three days later—on July 12, 1980—Chris and Rhonda exchanged spiritual vows in Los Angeles' Griffith Park, although his divorce from Sandy still wasn't final. But nothing could dim their spirits or cramp their style. Nearly every *General Hospital* cast member—including Jackie Zeman, John Beradino, and David Lewis—was on hand to help them celebrate their outdoor ceremony of love. Rhonda wore a beautiful designer wedding gown; Chris was dressed in a white tuxedo; and even his son, Chris, Jr., had flown in from Florida for the big event. In February 1982 Chris and Rhonda's first son, Shane Powhatan, was born; two years later, they welcomed another son, Coby James.

That marriage ended in 1985—the same year that Chris ran into trouble with Uncle Sam and the IRS. He was sentenced to four months in prison—and ordered to do 200 hours of community work—after pleading guilty to charges of income tax evasion. His lawyer argued that incarceration made no sense, since Chris needed to be able to keep working in order to pay back the $350,000 that he owed the government. The argument had merit, and Chris was remanded to Hollywood's Vinewood Prison, where he was detained only at night and on weekends. He was allowed to leave prison every morning at 5:35 A.M. to report to *General Hospital* and wasn't obligated to return to Vinewood until 11 P.M. Still, the experience left scars. "I'm guilty and I'm sorry," said Chris. "I've never done anything in my life that was as stupid and I've never paid for any mistake I've made like I've paid for this one."

BACKSTAGE
AFFAIRS

Whe doors slam and lights go out in dressing rooms in the middle of the day, it doesn't mean an actor needs a little privacy to practice his yoga. More likely than not, he's about to get into the missionary—not the lotus—position.

On the soaps, backstage love affairs are an occupational hazard. Co-stars who work together week after week—steaming up the screen as erotically as the network censors will allow—find it hard to turn off their feelings when the camera stops.

Sometimes a backstage entanglement leads to marriage; sometimes it leads to hell.

Knots Landing star Ted Shackelford was married to Jan Leverenz, a producer of educational films, for eight years. Then a twenty-seven-year-old Canadian actress named Teri Austin joined the cast. As Ted's character (restless playboy Gary Ewing) started putting the moves on Teri's character (mystery woman Jill Bennett), the plot thickened, both on-screen and off. Soon their setside affair became common knowledge, and Ted announced that he'd left his wife.

Even after the separation news broke, Ted and Teri continued to downplay their involvement. In September 1986 they both attended the star-studded Los Angeles premiere of the Sissy Spacek movie *'night Mother,* but Ted showed up with a pretty blonde named Catherine Carlen, and Teri's date was Mike Cutler. Nevertheless, the rumors didn't die down.

Sometimes it seems like Ted has actually lived the life he portrays on-screen. Aside from their mutual marital problems (Gary's left two wives—first Val, then Abby), both men are dedicated environmentalists, both

After Ted Shackelford and longtime wife Jan Leverenz broke up, he was linked with Knots Landing *costar Teri Austin.*

have an attraction for high-speed auto racing, and on a darker note, both are recovered alcoholics.

What draws costars together into such high-risk relationships? In the case of Ted Shackelford and Teri Austin, discontent had a great deal to do with it. Ted's marital wanderlust developed at a time when he'd come to a turning point in his life—a turning point that he wasn't quite ready to face. Ted was in his late thirties, his contract was up for renewal on *Knots Landing,* and though he'd often grumbled that he felt angry and frustrated at playing Gary Ewing—the show's perennial thin-skinned whipping boy—there wasn't much he could do about it. For better or for worse, after seven years in prime-time, *Knots Landing* defined him as a star. Without the show, he might find himself lucky to get a movie of the week or a guest spot on *Hotel* now and then. Patrick Duffy had learned that lesson the hard way during his sink-or-swim year off *Dallas.*

The character of Jill Bennett had originally arrived on *Knots Landing* to break up the marriage of Karen and Mac MacKenzie (Michele Lee and Kevin Dobson), but viewers refused to stand for that. So Jill was rerouted out of Mac's arms right into Gary's—and she instantly breathed new life into his character.

"Jill was the perfect cure for Gary Ewing's midlife crisis," says one setside observer, "and Teri came along at a time when Ted needed a little bolstering, too. She was a newcomer in Los Angeles, very much alone, and there weren't too many people in the cast she could hang out with. Joan Van Ark's married, Connie McCashin's married, Kevin Dobson, William Devane, and Doug Sheehan are all family people. It seemed like everybody else was either married or involved. So Ted became her friend. And when he found out she was a sports lover—and could shoot a pretty mean game of pool—well, that only intensified things."

Dallas' Victoria Principal, too, knows all about the dangers of a back-stage romance. In her case it led to a marriage that fell apart quicker than you can say Pamela Barnes Ewing. In 1979 Victoria started carrying on with Christopher Skinner, an actor who was hired for a bit part on *Dallas.* He was twenty-two—ten years younger than the gorgeous *Dallas* star—but the age difference didn't bother either of them. After their third date they eloped to Las Vegas and were married in a hasty civil ceremony with no guests present. "We didn't need anyone else there," Victoria assured the press. "The ceremony was a very personal commitment between the two of us."

But the honeymoon didn't last. Career conflicts soon darkened the horizon. In 1980—as *Dallas'* popularity soared—Victoria Principal's star rose with it; unfortunately, Christopher's didn't. There were money problems, too. At that point, Victoria was earning $10,000 a week on *Dallas;* they lived in an unpretentious house in one of the Beverly Hills canyons, but Victoria was anxious to move into a more luxurious love nest. Not that she'd actually be home much to furnish it. Victoria was clocking grueling seventy-five-hour weeks at the *Dallas* studio, which left her precious little time for a homelife or a husband. Most of all, she refused to sacrifice her career and become the kind of traditional wife, mother, and homemaker that Christopher wanted. Twenty months after their Las Vegas nuptials, they split up.

Traditional, of course, is hardly a word one would ever associate with Victoria Principal, especially where her love life is concerned. She started making headlines in that department long before she ever landed on *Dallas*. As a young Hollywood starlet, Victoria ricocheted her way through tempestuous affairs with Frank Sinatra, Elliott Gould, Desi Arnaz, Jr., Warren Beatty, George Peppard, and football star Lance Rentzel. She was known around town as a happy-go-lucky party girl, and it was anybody's guess whether she'd eventually rise to the top or sink to the bottom.

After her affair with Frank Sinatra, she was reportedly so distraught that she thought about suicide. Her three-year romance with British financier Bernard Cornfeld, which started in the late 1960s, was even more of a roller-coaster ride. Victoria met him while on a modeling assignment in London, quickly moved in with him, and became his mistress. Cornfeld showered her with expensive trinkets, including a Rolls-Royce, but passion turned to scandal when Victoria hauled him into court on charges of physical abuse. She alleged, among other things, that he'd tried to strangle her.

In 1971, following her bizarre breakup with Cornfeld, Victoria returned to the United States to take on her first major acting role—as Paul Newman's girlfriend in the movie *The Life and Times of Judge Roy Bean*. Off-screen, she continued to flit from one amorous leading man to the next, and her only brief intermission was her short-lived 1980 marriage to Christopher Skinner.

But when Skinner dropped out of her life, Victoria quickly climbed back on the roller-coaster and took up with rock star Andy Gibb, who was thirteen years her junior. Their initial meeting was a press agent's dream. While Gibb—a leading member of the famed Bee Gees singing group—was rehearsing an appearance on *The John Davidson Show*, he confessed to Davidson's staff that he had a secret crush on Victoria Principal. She was the only reason he bothered to watch *Dallas* every week. Coincidentally, she was practically within earshot when he made that confession. She happened to be guesting on *The Tonight Show*, which taped right next door to Davidson's studio.

And so, unbeknownst to Gibb, Davidson's staff arranged for Victoria to sneak over to their set and surprise her shy admirer on the air. During his on-tape interview with Gibb, Davidson casually dropped Victoria Principal's name into the conversation. Andy blushed a little—and that's when Victoria popped out from behind the curtains and gave him a big kiss on the neck!

Despite the gimmicky nature of their first encounter, they quickly became inseparable—and during their intense two-year involvement Andy encouraged her to sing (she even cut a record) and was a constant visitor on the *Dallas* set. But wild parties, reckless road tours, and drugs were all part of the rock-'n'-roll life-style—and eventually it was Andy's drug problem that forced Victoria to leave.

She went from that debacle into a much healthier relationship with Dr. Henry Glassman, a thirty-nine-year-old Beverly Hills plastic surgeon, whom she married in July 1985. Of course there had to be a few headlines connected with this new chapter in her life, too.

When Victoria first met Glassman, he was in the middle of a messy divorce. His embittered wife, Jane, was demanding a staggering financial settlement, which Glassman claimed he was unable to pay. By the time the case got to court, Victoria and Glassman were already living together and she became embroiled in the case, too. Glassman protested that he was in financial arrears. He owed back taxes and had accumulated numerous other debts. But Jane disputed his so-called poverty, pointing to the fact that he'd recently bought Victoria a huge, expensive diamond ring. That's when Victoria got into the act, maintaining that she'd paid for the ring herself. Finally, the court awarded Jane $7000 a month in alimony—a total of $84,000 a year. And despite his high-powered Beverly Hills medical practice, it looked like Henry Glassman was going to have to live on peanut butter and jelly sandwiches for a while to satisfy all his creditors. (Just in fighting his former wife, he'd run up a $110,000 legal tab.)

Dollar signs had a lot to do with matching up another pair of celebrity lovers, but in this instance winning money—not worrying over it—was the catalyst that brought them together. Their first date, if you can call it that, took place on the soundstage of the popular TV game show *$25,000 Pyramid*. Of course that's not where they originally started glancing—no, make that glaring—at each other.

It all began in 1978 when a brunette beauty queen named Brynn Thayer joined *One Life to Live*. She was taking over the part of Jenny Wolek, a missionary nun who'd recently ditched her habit—and her celibate life-style, too. Brynn's predecessor in the role, actress Kathy Glass, wasn't exactly a saint, either. She left the soap because she wanted more money than ABC was willing to shell out. So much for vows of poverty.

But Kathy Glass had been extremely popular in the role. In fact, according to the highly revered celebrity Q-rating system, she was at that time one of the top five actresses on soaps. No wonder Brynn—a former model and total novice at television acting—was shaking in her boots when she arrived at the ABC studio complex on Manhattan's West Sixty-sixth Street.

She soon made friends with some of the A-players on the show—Erika Slezak, Michael Storm, and Judith Light—but there was one actor who terrified her. That was Gerald Anthony, better known to *One Life to Live* fans as wild, impulsive Marco Dane. He was daytime's answer to Al Pacino—short, wiry, and explosive.

Backstage the real Gerald Anthony could be just as formidable. Even though he was a few inches shorter than Brynn, this man was an actor's actor—theatrical to the core—and she was just a wide-eyed girl from Texas who'd won a few beauty pageants and posed for magazine covers now and then. Jerry did nothing to put her at ease. "I was fearful of him right from the beginning," Brynn remembers. "I thought he was too brash, too aloof, and incredibly curt with people."

Jerry wasn't exactly charmed by her either. She had "Miss Congeniality" written all over her. She was just the type of girl he always steered clear of. She was too smiley, too cheery, too friendly to everybody on the set. She should be back home in Texas organizing prom weekends and decorating the sorority house, he thought, not trying to pass herself off as an actress. The dislike was so strong—and so distinctly mutual—that for months Brynn Thayer and Jerry Anthony went out of their way to avoid running into each other backstage. She liked to gossip in the makeup room during rehearsal breaks; he avoided the place like the plague. There were several local bars and restaurants on Columbus Avenue where the cast generally hung out after work. If Brynn went to one, almost by instinct (it seemed) Jerry would be sure to turn up at another.

Then fate intervened—in the form of Dick Clark—who needed some soap opera stars as guest celebrity players on *$25,000 Pyramid*. Dick Clark's office sent the message out to ABC, and ABC in turn asked Joe Stuart, producer of *One Life to Live,* to volunteer two of his actors. Jerry Anthony—a notorious game-show junkie—was naturally Joe's first choice. Now he had to find the right *Pyramid* partner for Jerry.

That's when the fun began. He asked Erika Slezak. She had other commitments. He tried Jacquie Courtney. She didn't care much for game shows. He begged Judith Light, who backed off, too. The thought of having to think fast on-screen gave her instant panic attacks. Finally, in desperation, Joe approached newcomer Brynn Thayer and asked—well, actually ordered—her to do *Pyramid*. "I knew I was a last-minute replacement," Brynn says, "but I was thrilled anyway—at first. Then a light bulb went off in my head. I said, 'Joe, who's going to do the show with me?' When I heard the name Jerry Anthony, I thought, 'What am I getting myself into? Let me out of here!' But I was afraid to say no to Joe Stuart. I was still the new girl on the block. So I figured I'd better grin and bear it. But I couldn't get Jerry out of my mind. I just kept walking around and thinking, 'Oh my God, am I gonna have to deal with this guy!' "

The next day Jerry knocked on Brynn's dressing room door. He just wanted to tell her how glad he was they'd be doing *Pyramid* together. Then he explained to her how important it was that their team win. Brynn was dumbfounded. She just stood there listening and nodding her head. Jerry suggested that they start getting together every night after work to practice the game. That way they'd have a better chance of winning on the air. Brynn thought he was crazy, but she didn't know how to say no. Jerry kept talking, Brynn kept listening, and pretty soon they had a date for eight o'clock that night to play *$25,000 Pyramid*. Well, not a date exactly. A coaching session to end all coaching sessions was more like it.

When Jerry showed up at her apartment, he came armed with five editions of the *$25,000 Pyramid* board game. They stayed up past midnight, playing the game, pacing, talking, laughing, munching on snacks, and doing round after endless round of word association until his eyes were bleary, her head was spinning, and they both couldn't think straight.

"I felt like I was in training for the Olympics," Brynn laughs, "but I quickly found out that's how Jerry is. He's incredibly competitive. When he goes after something, he really puts his heart and soul into it."

During that week-long marathon of *Pyramid* preparation, it was strictly work. At the time, Brynn and Jerry were both dating other people—and both having problems in their relationships—so in between rounds of *Pyramid* they wound up baring their souls a little. "We kind of became each other's psychiatrist," Brynn remembers.

The board game itself was a great ice-breaker, too. "Without realizing what was happening, we were getting acquainted through the process of word association," Brynn says. "For instance, I'd say hammer and Jerry would come back with a weird word like cantaloupe. I'd ask what in the world made him say that, and he'd start telling me some crazy story from his childhood, like the time his uncle tried to split open a cantaloupe with a hammer. Pretty soon we were laughing like a couple of lunatics and spilling out our whole life stories to each other."

By the end of the week the picture was definitely changing. "I remember looking at him late one night," Brynn says, "and suddenly seeing him in a whole new light. He was so intelligent, so deep, with all that crazy, restless energy of his. By midnight I'd be completely wiped out, but that's when Jerry would still be pacing up and down the room, raring to go. I remember looking at him and thinking, 'He's a really intricate person. Oh boy, I'd like to be with him. Oooh boy, what am I getting into here?' "

Those grueling nightly workouts paid off. During their week's stint on *$25,000 Pyramid,* Brynn and Jerry won $23,000, which they donated to the Save the Children foundation. The show was taped in Hollywood, and during their return flight to New York, they spent the entire five-and-a-half hours holding hands and talking animatedly, reliving every magic moment of their triumph. They came back to *One Life to Live* feeling flushed with victory and practically walking on air. Within a week, Jerry asked Brynn out on a formal date.

Brynn Thayer and Jerry Anthony, who wed and divorced during their One Life to Live *stint, are proof that some pyramids don't last forever.*

They remained backstage lovers for the next two years; then, in the fall of 1981 (after several breakoffs and reconciliations), they decided to get married.

The wedding was a small, private ceremony in Manhattan with several close pals from *One Life to Live* present, including Brynn's best friend, Judith Light. Shortly afterward the newlyweds bought a house in the country—complete with a dog named Larry and a duck named Willie—but still kept an apartment in Manhattan for stayovers on nights when taping at ABC ran late. Judith Light and her boyfriend, actor Robert Desiderio (whom she later married), often drove up to the country on weekends to help Brynn and Jerry plaster ceilings, polish floors, and hang wallpaper.

For a while Brynn and Jerry seemed like an ideal couple. Even their wedding had a storybook quality to it. The ceremony and reception took place on November 21, 1981, at Windows on the World restaurant in New York's World Trade Center. The view was breathtaking and the New York skyline gleamed like a toy city below them.

More than sixty guests—family, friends, and castmates—were on hand to witness the event. Brynn and her best buddy, Judith Light, had come to the restaurant by limousine. Jerry and his entourage arrived in another group of cars. Early that morning Judith had appeared on Brynn's doorstep carrying a bulging shopping bag; in it was something old, something new, something borrowed, and something blue for the bride to carry as she walked down the aisle. The "something new" was truly exquisite— a golden heart-shaped locket, a gift for Brynn to wear on her wedding day.

Brynn's bridal outfit was simple yet elegant. She wore a white silk blouse and a mauve and brown skirt with a handpainted petal design. Jerry was dressed in a light gray suit. Herb Hampshire, a friend from Aspen, Colorado, performed the ceremony. He'd written the unconventional wedding vows, but the words and thoughts were based on conversations Brynn and Jerry had had with him beforehand. "We'd already been living together for some time," Brynn later explained, "so our decision to get married was a reaffirmation, a statement to everyone of how much we loved each other. Herb incorporated our thoughts and feelings perfectly into what he wrote. I'll treasure those words forever."

Although the wedding had many traditional touches, in one way Brynn and Jerry broke with the past. They opted not to have a best man or maid of honor. Instead, Jerry's folks "stood up" for him, while Brynn's parents escorted her down the aisle and stood beside her during the ceremony. A strong contingent from *One Life to Live* was on hand to kiss the bride, tease the groom, and wish the couple well. Among the guests were Robin Strasser (Dorian), Steve Fletcher (Brad), Margaret Klenck (Edwina), and Tony Call (Herb). Stephen Schnetzer (Marcello) and Nancy Snyder (Katrina) held hands all through the ceremony. In short order, these backstage sweethearts would follow Brynn and Jerry's lead and become man and wife, too.

But whatever problems had existed before the marriage only began to multiply now. Actors in general have a hard time making a go of it—in Brynn and Jerry's case the conflicts became insurmountable. He was serious and intense; she was low-keyed and outgoing. Jerry lived, breathed, ate, and slept theater; Brynn was indelibly middle-class at heart. She wanted to shop at Bloomingdale's, lunch with friends, fix up the house. Worse yet, Brynn was a morning person who rose at the first sound of Jane Pauley's voice on the *Today* show. Jerry was a night owl who went into gear just when David Letterman was coming on. It was soon apparent that marriage—at least to each other—just wasn't their style. "They were much better cast as lovers than as husband and wife," one friend commented. "It was only a matter of time before things started going downhill."

At the end of 1982 Judith Light and Robert Desiderio left New York to try their luck in California. (Judith costarred with Tony Geary in the TV movie *Intimate Agony,* then made her real prime-time breakthrough as Tony Danza's costar on *Who's the Boss?*) When Judith vacated her *One Life to Live* dressing room, Brynn moved in with Robin Strasser. That was a small upheaval compared to what lay ahead. By this time Brynn and Jerry were living very separate lives. She was hanging out with her soap pals; he was devoting all his time and energy to a new business. He was trying to set himself up as a theatrical producer (in partnership with Jeff Fahey, the actor who played his kid brother, Gary Corelli, on *One Life*).

Professionally, Brynn and Jerry were both increasingly discontented on the soap and smarting over disappointments. In 1982 Jerry had been nominated for a supporting-actor Emmy; he lost to *General Hospital's* David Lewis. A year later the same thing happened to Brynn. She was nominated as best supporting actress, but the award went to Louise Shaffer (of *Ryan's Hope*).

According to a veteran setsider, "The Emmies weren't the real straw that broke the camel's back—it was the day-to-day tedium of doing the soap. At one point they'd both been extremely prominent characters on the show, but things changed radically, especially after Judith Light left. She was the glue that seemed to hold their storylines together. The show got new writers and started building new stars. Jerry's character, Marco Dane—once Llanview's answer to Tony Geary—seemed to be relegated more and more to the background. Brynn was suddenly playing step-mother to a teenager who was being groomed as the show's new heroine. Ridiculous as it sounds, she and Jerry were both old folks now, at least in the writers' eyes."

Apparently neither of them could leave their work worries at the studio. By the end of 1983 their conflicts had become so intense that they decided to separate. Jerry stayed on alone in their Connecticut country house with Willie the duck. Brynn moved back to Manhattan with Larry, their dog. The marriage had lasted just two years. In 1985 they both left *One Life to Live*. At the time, Brynn was plagued by family problems. (Her father, Paul Thayer, had recently been implicated in a national political scandal.) Later on, she moved to California and began getting prime-time work. Her most stand-out role to date came in the fall of 1986 when she starred as Bruce Willis' oversexed stepmother on the season opener of *Moonlighting*.

In 1984 singer/actress Gloria Loring found herself doing a little "moonlighting," too—in the form of a night-after-night rehearsing with her handsome young costar, Don Diamont. At the time, Gloria was playing the long-suffering Liz Curtis on *Days of Our Lives* and Don had just been hired to play Carlo Forenza, a South American freedom fighter who was supposed to wage his best campaigns on the bedsheets, not the battlefield. Gloria was thirty-seven; Don was twenty-one—but age wasn't their biggest obstacle. Gloria's domestic status was: she was still (technically, at least) married to actor/talk-show host Alan Thicke.

Apparently Gloria wanted to eat her cake and have it too. She became enraged when a daytime fan magazine delved into the nitty-gritty about her impending divorce from Alan Thicke (even though the magazine generously left out any mention of her very obvious romance with Diamont). In retrospect, though, it was a rough time for all concerned. *Days of Our Lives'* executive producer, Al Rabin, was so displeased with Diamont's listless performances that he consistently chewed him out in front of the cast. Alan Thicke's late-night talk-show, *In the Thicke of the Night*, was getting slaughtered in the ratings by Johnny Carson—and the offending magazine in question had cheerfully poured salt on the wounds. Their tongue-in-cheek title for the divorce story was, "In the Thicke of the Fight." But what irked Gloria most was that the writer of the article had called the separation "bitter."

She dashed off an angry letter to the magazine, declaring, "There's nothing bitter about our breakup. In fact, Alan and I are still living in the same house while all the legalities are being settled. My mother-in-law is living with us and helping take care of our children, Brendan and Robin. And my brother-in-law, Todd Thicke, is heading my new record album project. It's family first, and there is a spirit of cooperation and gentleness that is very poignant. Alan and I have worked very hard in trying to maintain our dignity and integrity at a very difficult time. We have tried to handle everthing responsibly. Nor do I think our marriage was a failure.

At a Days of Our Lives *cast party, Gloria Loring and Don Diamont stuck close together on the extreme right. At the time she was in the process of divorcing Alan Thicke.*

It succeeded far beyond what most people could have hoped for."

However, in her fury at the magazine, Gloria somehow managed to overlook two important details: (1) The editor had treated her very kindly, indeed, by keeping a tight lid on her sticky extramarital situation and (2) When the writer of the article had phoned to check out the facts about her separation, she had categorically denied having any marital problems at all—at the same time that Alan Thicke's publicist was releasing the breakup announcement to the press.

Actually, Alan and Gloria's divorce proceeded very smoothly indeed— far better, in fact, than *Days of Our Lives'* attempt to break up her on-screen marriage. Fans were appalled at the idea that Liz Curtis could be unfaithful to her adoring husband Neil (Joe Gallison), so the writers soon had some emergency rewriting to do. They arranged a hurried reconciliation scene between Liz and Neil and shipped Carlo off into permanent cold storage.

As a result, Don Diamont found himself on the unemployment line, but not out of Gloria Loring's life. In fact, as soon as it was legally possible,

he moved in with her and her two sons. She wasn't the first older woman
he'd been involved with. By his own admission, Don had been fixated on
women over thirty-five for some time. "In each case it happened not
because she was an older woman," he said, "but because of the person she
was. She could have been sixteen, but she happened to be thirty-five or
thirty-six or thirty-seven. Each time I just felt this incredible chemistry.
What could I do? It's nothing like those sex-oriented movies that Matt
Lattanzi and Rob Lowe make."

In the long run, though, all the parties in this tangled threesome
landed heads up. Gloria Loring's soap opera popularity never wavered;
Alan Thicke made a fabulous TV comeback in *Growing Pains,* a sitcom
that took the Nielsen ratings by storm; and Don Diamont didn't stay idle,
either. He found a much better soap slot for himself playing Brad Carl-
ton—an all-American go-getter—on *The Young and the Restless.*

Today, Don and Gloria can sit back in their well-guarded hilltop
Hollywood home—surrounded by children, dogs, swimming pool, and
Jacuzzi—and think to themselves, "All's well that ends well."

•   •   •

Happy endings have never exactly been in the cards for another *Days of
Our Lives* heroine, Deidre Hall. Professionally, Deidre's *Days* role as Dr.
Marlena Evans Brady has brought her to the pinnacle of the fan magazine
polls and kept her there for nine years, and in 1986 she even branched
out into her own prime-time show, *Our House,* with Wilford Brimley.
But romantically nothing ever seems to work out for her. Her marriage
to musician Keith Barbour ended in divorce in 1978. After that Deidre
was involved with *Lou Grant*'s Robert Walden, *Dynasty*'s Jack Coleman,
and Richard Dean Anderson (of *General Hospital* and *MacGyver* fame). At
one point she lost her heart to *Days* castmate Quinn Redeker (Alex Mar-
shall) who flew her all the way to Venice once, on a whim, for a romantic
weekend. But Redeker had just come through an emotionally draining
divorce after twenty years of marriage and he wasn't really in the market
for another round of domesticity.

In September 1984 Dee showed up on the *Days* set flashing a diamond
ring—a gift from television exec Steve Sohmer, who was then a vice
president at NBC. But the romance soured after a few months. By the
spring of 1985 Dee was telling the press, "Steve and I are no longer
engaged, but I hope we'll always be friends. He's a wonderful man and I
have no regrets. I'm just glad we realized that marriage wasn't for us before
we rushed into anything."

Right after her TV character, Marlena, married Roman (Drake Hogestyn), Deidre Hall made the switch to prime-time in Our House.

But it didn't take long for Deidre to bounce back. Within a month she already had a new love—a bruiser named Joe, who was definitely the strong, silent type. True, her latest Romeo was more of a hulk than a hunk, but her feelings for him were very sincere. They met guesting on a prime-time entertainment show.

Work kept throwing them together. In the course of preparing for the show, they had to rehearse for weeks and weeks—understandably so, since they had a rather difficult stunt to execute.

The show, you see, was *Circus of Stars* and Joe was a performing elephant. When Deidre climbed on his trunk, he had to flip her onto his back.

Deidre came away from that relationship with a few sore muscles, but no regrets. Their joint acrobatic debut was a huge success, and later it was hard to say goodbye. "Joe was a lot nicer than some of the animals on two legs who prowl the L.A. singles scene," sighed Deidre with just the slightest hint of sarcasm in her voice. "He even purred if you hugged him. And it didn't take much to make him happy. Just give him some peanuts or his favorite treat—a bagel—and he'd be your friend for life."

THE
DYNASTY
DOLLS

O n *Magnum P.I.* Tom Selleck dotes on his red Ferrari; on *Miami Vice* Don Johnson cuddles up with his pet alligator, Elvis. Neither one of them can sustain a decent long-term relationship, but it's okay. They're hunks—and the women in their lives are strictly window dressing. In a sense, the real stars of the show are the car chases and the shoot-outs.

But soaps are a different story. While detective dramas glorify the caveman ethic, soap operas have always been a women's medium. From Stella Dallas to Erica Kane—from Our Gal Sundae to Our Miss Ellie—every serial comes complete with its own version of Cinderella, a wicked witch, and a fairy godmother.

Nowhere is that game plan more in evidence than on *Dynasty,* where Cinderella (Krystle) is married to her rich, handsome prince (Blake), but constantly thwarted by the evil witch (Alexis) who wants to destroy them both. Looming in the background is Blake's half-caste sister, Dominique, a mysterious outsider (who's independently wealthy—just like any self-respecting fairy godmother would be). Whenever Blake and Krystle come too close to the brink, she's always there to bail them out with tea, tax-deductible bonds, and sympathy.

Off-screen, Linda Evans, Joan Collins, and Diahann Carroll—*Dynasty*'s three reigning furies—are often locked in combat, too. Joan Collins and Linda Evans don't exactly greet each other with hugs and kisses; they're about as chummy as Alexis and Krystle. Whenever the two stars have to make a joint personal appearance, the situation gets tense. On cross-country publicity junkets, the show routinely requests that the two stars never be given adjoining plane seats—or hotel suites on the same floor.

A few years ago a TV awards appearance nearly turned into a sequin-gowned version of *The Three Stooges,* when Linda Evans, Joan Collins, and Diahann Carroll were all asked to co-present the same award. Apparently Joan was determined to stand out—in the center of the group—but when they reached the podium, Diahann turned the tables on her by moving all the way to the right, leaving Linda in the middle. On *Dynasty* shenanigans like that are par for the course.

There's never been any love lost between *Dynasty*'s star blonde and star brunette, but things really came to a head in the summer of 1985 when Joan Collins refused to show up for work. The cast was all set to start filming the season opener—the resolution of the bloodbath in Moldavia—but Joan was still in tenuous contract negotiation with the show and holding out for more money. In the first episode she was supposed to be taken hostage and chained in a dungeon by the Moldavian insurrectionists, but because she was unavailable for work, Krystle—not Alexis—wound up being sent to the storm cellar. And Linda Evans found herself playing out a storyline originally intended for another actress—hardly an ideal situation.

As the season progressed, what rankled even more was the fact the "Krystle kidnapped" storyline—in which Linda Evans played both Krystle and Rita, her lowlife look-alike—did nothing but help sink the ratings. When the writers finally moved Krystle off the front burner—and brought Alexis back to the fore, spewing more venom than ever—the show vaulted into the winners' circle again.

That kind of defeat was hard for Linda Evans to take—and Joan Collins' new role as *Dynasty*'s "savior" certainly didn't endear her to Linda or the rest of the cast. She ran into problems with other *Dynasty* stars—especially Diahann Carroll. Joan wasn't particularly thrilled by the birth of *Dynasty*'s stepchild—*The Colbys.* Fearing that it might dilute the strength of her own show, she urged the rest of the cast to boycott *The Colbys* and refuse to do any guest appearances on it. John Forsythe didn't listen and neither did Diahann Carroll, who became soaps' first commuting star, traveling back and forth between *Dynasty* and *The Colbys,* during the spin-off's first season.

Diahann, of course, isn't accustomed to taking orders from anyone—especially not from someone like Joan Collins, who was grinding out tacky grade-B movies when Diahann was a Broadway star and one of the top

Dynasty's Dominique Deveraux and Alexis Dexter are archenemies. Off-screen, Diahann Carroll and Joan Collins have their moments, too.

nightclub entertainers in America. Diahann's always marched to the beat of her own drum. She's as wily and independent as Dominique Deveraux, the jet-set chanteuse she plays on *Dynasty*. She was born Carol Johnson (Diahann's her middle name) and grew up in Harlem, but made up her mind as a young girl to break out of the ghetto. Her father, a New York

City subway conductor, and her mother, a nurse, encouraged her singing and acting ambitions; and by the time she was fifteen, Diahann was already taking on professional modeling assignments.

During her one year of study at New York University, Diahann earned tuition money working in nightclubs around the city—then she dropped out of college to accept a featured role in the Dorothy Dandridge/Harry Belafonte movie *Carmen Jones*. She also earned glowing notices in the Broadway musical *House of Flowers,* but in those days—before productions like *Raisin* and *The Wiz* changed the color of things on the Great White Way—there were few Broadway roles for black entertainers. In 1958 Richard Rodgers almost hired Diahann to play the ingenue in his new musical, *Flower Drum Song.* But the girl was supposed to be Chinese-American, and even with several layers of makeup on, she simply didn't look believable in the part, so she lost out to Pat Suzuki. Rodgers kept her in mind, though, and in 1961 created another musical, *No Strings,* especially for her. The show, dealing head-on with interracial romance, was considered a theatrical landmark, and Diahann won a coveted Tony award for her compelling performance as a successful black model, living in Paris, who refuses to leave Europe and give up her career for the love of a white man (Richard Kiley).

By that time Diahann's own life was even more provocative. In 1956 she married her white talent manager, Monty Kay. (Diahann's family was so shocked that her father didn't attend the wedding even though it was held at the Abyssinian Baptist Church in Harlem.) The union produced a daughter, Suzanne, now twenty-six, but when Diahann landed a supporting role in the blockbuster movie musical *Porgy and Bess,* she became involved off set with Sidney Poitier, the film's leading man. In 1961 her marriage ended. Poitier had already divorced his wife to be with Diahann, but once they were both free, their affair didn't last long. Her next major passion—in the early 1970s—was another entertainer, British talk-host David Frost. Their engagement made banner headlines and lasted three years. But her relationships with Frost, like her liaison with Poitier, somehow never culminated in marriage.

Diahann did marry, though, on the rebound. Just a few weeks after breaking up with David Frost, she eloped with Fredde Glusman, a Caucasian Las Vegas businessman. They were divorced within four months. Then in 1975 she married for yet a third time. The groom was a black magazine editor named Robert DeLeon, and this desperate attempt at happiness proved to be even more bittersweet in its own way than any of her others. Diahann once described DeLeon, who was fifteen years her junior, as "a tragic figure" with undisclosed problems that she chose to ignore. Their two years together as man and wife were frequently turbulent. Then on March 31, 1977, DeLeon was killed while speeding in his Ferrari not far from their Beverly Hills home.

For a long time afterward Diahann lived in a kind of limbo, both professionally and personally. She felt her greatest triumphs were behind her. In 1974 she'd earned an Academy Award nomination for her performance as a welfare mother with six kids in *Claudine,* but her film career had never really taken off after that. In the late 1960s, her TV sitcom, *Julia,* had enjoyed a respectable three-year run, but the experience had been a mixed bag for her. Critics complained that *Julia*—TV's first black comedy-heroine—wasn't truly representative of black realities in America. With her "whitebread attitudes" and neat little middle-class life-style, critics harped that Julia was really a white woman masquerading as a black. Diahann bridled at such snipes. "People don't expect Marlo Thomas to be a spokeswoman for the Lebanese," she shot back.

After *Julia,* Diahann was leery of doing TV again. All through the 1970s she concentrated on her nightclub career—and took whatever decent roles came her way (which, for talented black actresses, were still few and far between). In 1983 she replaced Elizabeth Ashley in the haunting Broadway drama *Agnes of God.* It was a particularly satisfying acheivement for Diahann because not a single word of dialogue was rewritten when she stepped into the role; for once it truly didn't matter whether the character was supposed to be black or white.

But once her run in *Agnes of God* finished, Diahann went into a slump. It was the low that always followed the high of achieving something professionally and sustaining it. She missed having the theater to go to every night. She missed the work and the people and the applause. Sitting home alone, she got into the habit of watching TV and—in her need to escape from the sudden emptiness in her own life—became particularly addicted to the prime-time soaps. That's when the idea came to her— what shows like *Dynasty* and *Falcon Crest* were missing was a touch of color. "I found myself fascinated with these bitchy women like Joan Collins and Jane Wyman," Diahann remembers, "and I thought how marvelous it would be to work on a glamorous show like *Dynasty.* So I decided I'd be the first black bitch on prime-time TV. I called my business manager and told him. 'Be sure and let Aaron Spelling know exactly how I feel.' "

Spelling was interested, but the wheels were grinding exceedingly slow—a little too slow for Diahann's taste. Finally she decided to take matters into her own hands. On the night of the 1984 Golden Globe

Awards in Hollywood, Diahann was introduced to Spelling (she was there to sing a Barbra Streisand song from *Yentl*), and afterward Diahann decided to crash a private party that Spelling and his *Dynasty* entourage were holding at Touch, an exclusive L.A. nightclub. Her entrance was unforgettable—in fact, it was like a scene right out of *Dynasty:* Diahann slithered into the room, dripping furs and diamonds and dazzling everyone in sight. Spelling and his chief cohort, Esther Shapiro, realized that Diahann was doing an unsolicited audition for them, but it worked. They'd found just what they'd been looking for—the perfect match for Alexis Colby.

Diahann's starting salary ($35,000 an episode) was considerably less than Joan Collins', but her presence on the set still represented a potential threat—at least from the point of view of a certain other fiftyish brunette. Just what *Dynasty* needed was a sleek rich bitch who might put Alexis out of business—especially considering how the cards were stacked. Diahann was slightly younger, and just as shapely, as Joan. Moreover, she was a rather prestigious addition to the show. Diahann's last TV series, *Julia,* had brought her several Emmy nominations. She also had a Tony award to her credit—and an Oscar nomination—plus a high-powered singing career. Joan, for all her glitz and gloss, had been reduced to making films like *Empire of the Ants, The Stud,* and *The Bitch* before *Dynasty* retrieved her from the lower depths.

Still and all, Joan was charming—at least publicly—when Diahann first arrived on the set. The cold war came later. But Diahann had little time to fret about territorial skirmishes. She was too busy making a simultaneous comeback in another area of her life. At that time, she was embarking on a new romantic involvement, her first in many years. In the spring of 1984 Diahann had just started dating nightclub singer Vic Damone, fifty-seven, whom she'd met when they were performing at the same hotel in Palm Beach, Florida. Music wasn't their only link—Damone's personal life was as tattered as hers. His marriage to actress Pier Angeli lasted exactly four years (she later remarried, then committed suicide after a long battle with drugs and depression). Damone's second wife, Judy Rawlins, followed much the same pattern, becoming addicted to drugs and eventually killing herself. The singer's third marriage, to Rebecca Ann Jones, simply ended in divorce when she couldn't get along with his four children.

Diahann and Vic seemed determined not to repeat the past. With six strikes between them, they knew, in their case, marriage was a risky venture at best; still, by the summer of 1986, they found themselves quietly drifting toward it. If Diahann was stepping into possibly dangerous waters again, whom could she ask for guidance? She certainly couldn't look to either of her *Dynasty* costars for domestic advice. Linda Evans and Joan Collins would hardly qualify as experts on the subject of marital longevity.

Linda Evans was born in Hartford, Connecticut—her real name is Linda Evenstad—but her family migrated to North Hollywood, California, when she was six months old. Both her parents were dancers, but her father became a housepainter and decorator to support his wife and three daughters. Linda attended Hollywood High—a school that also turned out Stefanie Powers, Tuesday Weld, and Carol Burnett—but her teenage years were hardly idyllic. Linda, who was tall for her age, felt awkward and uncomfortable—especially around boys. And there were family problems at home. When she was fifteen her father died after a long battle with cancer.

Her father's death affected her deeply, and she may have been searching for a replacement "father figure" when, at the age of twenty-five, she married John Derek, who was sixteen years her senior. Derek made a career out of marrying beautiful women and then molding them to his will—Ursula Andress was Linda's predecessor; Bo Derek succeeded her. In each instance Derek enjoyed playing Svengali.

Linda was so in awe of him that she gladly gave up her independence. During their marriage, Derek controlled nearly every part of her life. He chose her clothes, her hairstyle, made all her career decisions. She basically existed only in his shadow.

By the time she married John, Linda had already been an actress for ten years, but success had only been sporadic. As a teenager, she'd actually worked with her future *Dynasty* costar John Forsythe for the first time when she made an appearance on his TV sitcom, *Bachelor Father*. Forsythe later remembered her as talented and appealing, but somehow that wasn't enough. Despite her beauty and ambition, stardom eluded her all through her twenties. After finishing high school, Linda made TV commercials, modeled, and occasionally did small roles in films like 1963's *Twilight of Honor*. Her big break didn't come until she landed the part of Barbara Stanwyck's daughter on *The Big Valley*, which ran from 1965 to 1969.

Even that didn't elevate her to A-player status in Hollywood. In fact, when Linda auditioned for a part on *Dallas* ten years later, she was turned down because the producers thought she was too old.

Part of the reason her career never caught fire was undoubtedly the influence of John Derek. When Linda married him, she became a wife first—and an actress second. When they met in 1965, his second wife, Scandinavian sex symbol Ursula Andress, had just dumped him for Jean-

Paul Belmondo, the leading French matinee idol of the 1960s. Derek was not only nursing a wounded ego, he was also an actor whose career was on the decline—but Linda was oblivious to all that. She remembered him from his Hollywood heyday; in fact, as a young girl Linda had idolized him. She'd even kept pictures of him on her bedroom wall.

Fantasy played a big part in their romance, and later in their marriage, too. Linda once described their life together to a reporter from *Orange Coast* magazine: "One night I came home to a roomful of candles," she said. "John had moved a mattress in front of a roaring fire in the living room and had furs spread on top. Champagne and grapes dipped in egg whites and dusted in sugar were nearby. It was marvelous."

But Linda paid a price for that Cinderella existence. After their wedding in 1967, she gave up her Hollywood career to move to Europe with John, and she agreed not to work in films unless they could work together. She also took on the arduous task of becoming a stepmother to John's son and daughter from his first marriage. It was a particularly difficult situation because, when Linda married him, John barely had any relationship at all with his kids. But Linda worked hard to change that, and she succeeded. Her stepdaughter, Sean Derek, later told *Los Angeles Times* writer Bettijane Levine, "My brother and I didn't know my father at all when he married Linda. Linda literally introduced us to him and helped us have a relationship."

During those years in Europe, when she was strictly Mrs. John Derek, Hollywood literally forgot about her. Her acting jobs were few and far between, and one of Linda's only American appearances was in a seminude layout in *Playboy* magazine. Her husband, John, who'd previously photographed Ursula Andress nude for *Playboy,* took the pictures.

But in 1973 their too-close-for-comfort relationship came to a not-so-snappy ending. John was on location in Greece filming *And Once Upon a Time* and became infatuated—on and off the set—with a sixteen-year-old actress named Bo Collins. To many observers, the resemblance was uncanny—she looked like a younger version of Linda Evans. Four years later, after divorcing Linda, John married his new "discovery" and proceeded to mold her into Bo Derek—the perfect "10"—the new pinup girl of the eighties.

In an interview with *McCall's,* Linda described her battle to save her marriage—and the futility of it all. "I thought if I gave him enough time, he would come to his senses and realize that it was impossible for him to be with this *child.* . . . I was sure John would come back to me—even after he and Bo were living together, John kept calling me and telling me he still loved me, but that he was very confused."

Krystle and Alexis' swimming-pool brawl was a Dynasty *classic. Actually, Linda Evans (who's athletic) enjoys the fight scenes far more than Joan Collins (who'd rather have a verbal duel).*

When Linda finally accepted the reality of the breakup, she came back to California and tried to get on with her life. She began dating an old friend, Stan Herman, who was a multimillionaire real estate tycoon. He was also a permanent fixture on the Hollywood party scene—and seven years older than Linda. Their marriage, which took place a year before John Derek wed Bo, lasted only a few years. It broke up when Linda announced her intention of resuming her acting career again.

In both cases Linda managed to accomplish a "civilized" divorce. In fact, her divorces were more than just civilized—they were downright sociable. To this day, Linda is friends with both of her ex-husbands and their new wives (Bo Derek and Denise Herman). And John's other ex, Ursula Andress, has even houseguested at Linda's on occasion.

If Linda seems philosophical about her marital failures, it's merely—as she puts it—because "it feels too horrible" to dwell on all that rejection. So instead she refuses to let herself be depressed and bitter. "When you do get to the other side of the pain," she says, "you can see yourself and others in a completely different way."

Stardom came late to Linda. She was nearly forty when *Dynasty* premiered and finally made her a star. Suddenly, after so many years of being overlooked, she was being acknowledged as one of the world's most beautiful women. It was a hard transition for her to make. Over and over again she told the press that she wouldn't trade anything to be twenty-two again—that she thought women became much more interesting with age—but she voiced one major regret about the state of her life: her childlessness. True, her good friend Ursula Andress had given birth to a healthy baby at the age of forty-four, but in Linda's case the right candidate for fatherhood just didn't seem to be on the horizon. For a while she dated George Santo Pietro, a Los Angeles restaurateur, and later she became involved with Richard Cohen, a fifty-year-old business magnate, but neither romance led to anything permanent. Cohen was so anxious to marry Linda that he built a $10-million mansion, complete with movie theater and health spa, hoping it would be their honeymoon house, but she turned him down. Maybe she's just been burned too many times to risk getting hurt again.

■   ■   ■

Joan Collins has made a career out of playing with fire. As a young starlet in London, Joan fell head over heels in love with actor Laurence Harvey. The suave, debonair film star introduced her to champagne and caviar and let her wander in the glittering, jet-set circle he traveled in, but their friendship never moved from the baccarat table to the bedroom.

Joan was mystified. She'd done everything she could to win him, yet Harvey continued to keep a gentlemanly distance. At the time, what she didn't know was that Harvey was actually living with another woman—middle-aged actress Hermione Baddeley—who was extremely possessive. When she and Joan finally met at a party, Baddeley instantly cut her down, snidely informing Joan that she had neither the looks nor the talent to ever succeed as a cinema actress. Joan didn't let those remarks stop her.

Baddeley, of course, was getting older and was painfully aware that she was starting to lose her own looks. She was frightened that Joan would steal her fair-haired boy. But in point of fact she had nothing to worry about. Harvey—for reasons known only to himself—never touched her. When their friendship ended, she was just as virginal as ever.

But the next man in her life—actor Maxwell Reed—was hardly that tender or considerate. In her autobiography, *Past Imperfect,* Joan paints him as loathsome and abusive. Yet, at the time she married him, she apparently had no inkling of his darker side, or maybe, in her girlish rapture, she simply chose to overlook all his negative qualities.

According to Joan, their honeymoon in Cannes was a nightmare from beginning to end. Max made Hermione Baddeley look like the world's most understanding lover. He would become irrationally jealous of any man who paid his wife the slightest bit of innocent attention. Yet there was something that consumed him even more than jealousy—greed. Joan claims he was willing to do anything for money—he even tried to sell her to an Arabian sheikh for one night of love. Joan was mortified when Max made that suggestion one evening when they were dining at Les Ambassadeurs, a posh London cabaret. In the middle of dinner, he introduced her to Sheikh Abdul Ben Kafir, then whispered that the sheikh was ready to pay 10,000 pounds for her sexual services. Max, it seemed, had already negotiated the deal on her behalf. He was ecstatic. Not only would the money be their passport to America (which he knew was Joan's greatest ambition), but the sheikh was even willing to let Max watch while he made love to his wife!

Joan stormed out of the restaurant—and out of Maxwell Reed's life forever. In her autobiography, she writes him off with a far from restrained adieu: "Not only did I not love him anymore," reveals Joan, "his sexual tendencies were increasingly sadistic and perverted."

Her own tastes were much simpler—she was far more interested in adulation than copulation. Joan was already a British film star when she'd married Reed, but she was virtually unknown outside the United Kingdom. In the wake of her divorce, she set out to establish herself as a Hollywood commodity, and in 1955 *The Girl in the Red Velvet Swing,* with Ray Milland and Farley Granger, did just that for her. While Marilyn Monroe reigned as America's Blond Bombshell, Joan became the sexiest brunette on-screen at the neighborhood drive-in.

During the 1950s Joan concentrated on her rising American film career. In short order she made *Sea Wife* with Richard Burton, *Island in the Sun* with James Mason, *Stopover Tokyo* with Robert Wagner, and *Rally Round the Flag, Boys!* with Paul Newman.

Joan didn't marry again until 1963. This time she chose a man who was gentle and sensitive—the total opposite of Maxwell Reed. He was

After shedding several leading men, Joan Collins seems to have found the perfect screenmate in Michael Nader. Off-screen, she's been married four times.

also extremely creative. The man she fell in love with was composer/actor/director Anthony Newley. Like Joan, he was British, half Jewish, and, unfortunately, just as volatile as she was. When their affair began, Tony was still married to actress Anne Lynn, whom he'd been separated from for three years. Until he met Joan the technicalities of his legal situation hadn't interested him at all, but now he couldn't wait to rush the divorce through so he could marry Joan. As soon as they were man and wife the newlyweds took up residence in New York, where Tony was starring in *Stop the World—I Want to Get Off!* Later they went to California where Tony immersed himself in filmmaking. Joan mainly concentrated on raising their children, Tara and Sacha.

But domesticity has never been her style. After a few brief years the charm of it all began to wear off and Joan wasn't content just to be Mrs. Anthony Newley. She missed the excitement of having a thriving career of her own. Meanwhile, Tony was consumed by work and riding high. They clashed constantly. On top of that, Tony's overbearing mother was a constant thorn in Joan's side. Eventually Joan and Tony agreed to go their separate ways and during the last years of their union, their life together was merely an uneasy truce. But Joan was still legally married when she became enamored of Ron Kass, the man who ran the Beatles' music company and later became president of MGM Records.

In 1970 Joan divorced Tony; a year later she married Ron, and their daughter, Katyana, was born in 1972. But all the same trouble spots that had plagued her previous marriage—money problems, constant bickering, Joan's frustration at her deteriorating career—began to eat away at her relationship with Ron.

In 1981 *Dynasty* catapulted Joan Collins back into the limelight, but it did nothing to improve her personal life. Even though *Dynasty* had suddenly transformed her from has-been to superstar, the marriage was over. Had she learned any lessons? Maybe; maybe not. This time Joan stayed single for less than three years. In 1985 she married Peter Holm, a much younger man, who shared the executive reins with her at the helm of her new TV production company, but the marriage lasted less than two years.

Joan and Peter's only producing venture was the 1986 CBS miniseries *Sins,* which teamed her with James Farentino and Timothy Dalton. The title, short and bittersweet, seemed like the perfect description of the actress' own life—and Joan would be the first to admit it. That's not to say she's sampled every piece of forbidden fruit on the Hollywood vine yet. But give her time. She's only fifty-three.

BARING THEIR ALL
AND OTHER
SKELETONS
IN THE CLOSET

*I*s there anyone alive who doesn't have something to hide? The stars who play saints and supermen on the soaps are really no different from the janitors who sweep their dressing rooms and the lackeys who shine their shoes. They're human, just like everybody else. If you rattle around in their closets, a few skeletons—and scandals—are bound to tumble out.

■   ■   ■

Burt Reynolds made newsstand history when he took his clothes off for *Cosmopolitan* magazine, but he certainly wasn't the first—or the last—actor to peddle his anatomy for fun and profit.

Steve Bond, who plays Jimmy Lee Holt on *General Hospital*, once posed nude for *Playgirl* magazine, and eight years later, when he became a soap opera superstud, *Playgirl* reprinted those X-rated photos in an attempt to cash in on the actor's newfound popularity.

At first Steve joked, "I knew I should have listened to my mother. She begged me not to do it." Later, he explained why he'd agreed to step out of his Jockey shorts—and into the limelight—in the first place. "Look, I was an out-of-work actor struggling to survive in Hollywood," he said. "I took my clothes off for the camera for one reason only—I needed the money. Maybe it was wrong, but I went for the cash—so I could pay the rent, keep on going to acting lessons and auditions, keep on working at my craft. But now I've learned that you've got to live with your past.

Years after he paraded in the buff, those nude photos still haunted General Hospital's *Steve Bond.*

Whatever you do comes back to haunt you. In a way, though, it's a relief. I've lived with this for eight years. Now it's all out in the open. I don't have any secrets anymore."

■   ■   ■

Shannon Tweed was never that modest about her physical attributes. When she auditioned for the part of Diana Hunter on *Falcon Crest,* she walked into the rehearsal room and instantly caught the casting director's eye. She was wearing a tight, clingy blouse—partially unbuttoned—and no bra. She opened up her portfolio and took out a pile of nude photos— mementos of her days as a *Playboy* centerfold. Although a slew of other actresses had already tested for the part, Shannon—with little acting experience—was hired at a starting salary of $15,000 a week.

Her *Falcon Crest* stint lasted only a year, but then she moved on to a new stint: Savannah Wilder—Josh Taylor's leading lady—on *Days of Our Lives.* Her arrival set off a few fireworks. The show's other blond bombshells were wary of the competition, but Shannon had no trouble holding her own. After all, she'd been taking care of herself since she was a teenager. Back in Saskatoon, Canada, she'd worked in nightclubs while still going to high school and even had cosmetic surgery when she was eighteen. She later became a top Canadian model, moved to the U.S., became romantically involved with *Playboy* publisher Hugh Hefner, and after that arrangement petered out, moved in with rock star Gene Simmons of Kiss fame. Hardly an apple-pie existence, but she's nothing if not totally honest (right down to the fact that she's had her breasts enlarged twice). She also admits that her relationship with Simmons was lust at first sight. "The minute I saw him, I wanted to go to bed with him," she said.

■　　■　　■

And then there's the actor who really got caught with his pants off. Ken Jezek, who plays Lars Englund on *Days of Our Lives,* was working on his tan on a Los Angeles beach—and wearing only the flimsiest g-string bikini. He was lying in the sand rump-up, and from that angle it appeared—at least to a passing police officer—that Ken wasn't wearing anything at all. The officer came over and demanded that Ken vacate the beach.

　　Ken wasn't alone. He was sharing a beach blanket with a pretty brunette named Karen Kelly, who plays Brenda Clegg on another soap, *Capitol.* She was outraged by the policeman's insinuations that she and

Left: *Shannon Tweed may be the most candid star in Hollywood. The former girlfriend of Hugh Hefner, she admits she's had her breasts enlarged twice—and that her current romance was "lust at first sight."* Right: Days of Our Lives' *Ken Jezek sometimes seems a little underdressed for success.*

her sand-castle Romeo were making a public spectacle of themselves, and she told the officer exactly what she thought. He proceeded to give her a summons for causing a scene. The whole thing made banner headlines in several publications that week—and everyone got a big chuckle out of Ken Jezek's beach blanket bust. Well, maybe not everyone. His wife, Evelyne, wasn't too pleased.

* * *

Speaking of headlines: in the summer of 1985, Mark Pinter—an actor on *As the World Turns*—became the father of twins. Knowing that heart-warming features always sell, *Daytime TV* magazine was eager to splash the story all over the cover, but time was of the essence. Since there were no pictures available of Mark, his wife Gretchen, and their brand-new son, Dylan, and daughter, Hannah, the magazine had to settle for a cover shot of Mark and his *As the World Turns* leading lady, Colleen Zenk. That, of course, presented a problem, since the accompanying feature had nothing to do with their TV characters, Brian McColl and Barbara Sten-beck. The subject was strictly Mark's nouveau fatherhood. So the editors came up with a headline that read: MARK PINTER BECOMES THE FATHER OF TWINS—AND COLLEEN ZENK'S THRILLED FOR HIM!

Shortly after leaving their mates, Mark Pinter and Colleen Zenk made their first public appearance together at an As the World Turns *cast party.*

As it turned out, "thrilled" wasn't exactly the right word—although Colleen certainly turned out to be a major force in rocking the Pinter family cradle. Before either of the twins had cut his or her first tooth, Mark left his wife, four-year-old daughter, Siri, brand-new babies, and brand-new house in Connecticut to spend much of his free time with Colleen and her two-year-old daughter, Kelsey.

In this case, probably the only people who were really thrilled were the lawyers who handled Mark's divorce from Gretchen and Colleen's divorce from actor Michael Crouch.

■   ■   ■

Lisa Peluso—a young actress who played Wendy Wilkins on *Search for Tomorrow*—had nothing to hide when she celebrated her nineteenth birthday at New York's trendy disco Magique. Her family and friends were all on hand for the big blow-out, and Lisa's boyfriend—a Chippendale's-style male dancer—decided to put on a show they'd never forget.

He ran up on stage, started gyrating seductively, and disrobed down to bikini briefs while the band played a rowdy rock tune. Then, as a special birthday tribute to the woman he loved, he produced something resembling a huge, glowing birthday candle from right between his legs.

Later, though, he got a trifle miffed when one magazine, in reporting the incident, referred to him as a "stripper" instead of a male entertainer. After all, anyone can wriggle out of his clothes to a raunchy beat, but to pull a big surprise out of his underwear—that's the hard part!

■   ■   ■

And there's always room for a little exhibitionism on every soap set. Take the case of boffo (no, make that buff-o) performer Michael O'Leary, who plays Dr. Rick Bauer on *The Guiding Light*. One day Michael was doing a shower scene with a brand-new actress on the show, Mary Kay Adams, who was playing the exotic India von Halkein. Mary Kay was supposed to walk into the bathroom, open the shower door, and shriek a little when she discovered Michael inside. All day they rehearsed it, with Michael standing in the shower with a towel wrapped around him. But during final taping Michael (who was only visible on-screen from the waist up) decided to improvise a bit. When Mary Kay Adams opened the shower door, there he was stark naked—wearing nothing but his boyish all-American grin. The scream she let out nearly broke the klieg lights.

■   ■   ■

Hunt Block, who plays Peter Hollister on *Knots Landing,* is severely allergic to sunlight. Even artificial lights, if they're bright enough, can induce a frenzied fit of sneezing—and probably no place is more brightly lit than the soundstage of a television show just before filming.

When Hunt arrived on *Knots Landing,* he was terrified of one thing—

sneezing in his leading lady's face. "I had visions of standing nose to nose with Donna Mills," he says, "and starting to itch and twitch like that prom queen with the roses in the old Dristan commercial. In my mind I could hear the director yelling, 'Cut! Cut! Somebody wipe that kid's nose, for Godsakes!' "

To keep from embarrassing himself in front of Donna Mills, Teri Austin, William Devane, or any of the other *Knots Landing* actors he had to work with, Hunt came up with a fail-safe allergy treatment. Every week just before filming, he'd sit in his dressing room and stare directly into a light bulb for half an hour. "It helped acclimatize my eyes to the light and I'd get all my sneezing out before I went on set," he says. Then he was free to commit hanky-panky without so much as reaching for a hanky.

■   ■   ■

Knots Landing's Donna Mills follows a strict diet—high-protein, low-sugar—because she suffers from hypoglycemia. When her blood-sugar level dips too low she's prone to mood swings that can darken an entire set. Donna jokes that if she eats one candy bar, she's ready to contemplate suicide, but the illness itself is no laughing matter. Her moods can affect her work and play havoc with her personal life, which isn't the most stable situation to begin with. For seven years she's been involved with rock guitarist Richard Holland, who moves in and out of her million-dollar-plus Benedict Canyon home as frequently as Donna changes eye makeup. Holland is six years younger than Donna (he's thirty-five; she's forty-one) and he's also the father of a seven-year-old son, Damien, from his marriage to rock singer Chaka Khan. By even the flimsiest calculations, Donna's been intimately involved with Holland since practically the day his son was born—but mentioning that fact is likely to make Donna's blood boil.

■   ■   ■

Despite the fame and fortune that comes with TV success, many stars become prone to serious depression. Take the case of a talented spitfire named Leslie Graves. In 1982 she was cast as the original Brenda Clegg— a spoiled rich girl on *Capitol*—and from the moment she walked on screen, she smoldered like Pia Zadora in pigtails. In order to play Brenda, Leslie had to make herself up to look fifteen, but in reality she was twenty-three years old and had enough hard knocks behind her to give Joan Collins a run for her money.

Brenda had been in the business since she was old enough to write her name. She got her TV start at age five on *Sesame Street,* but Leslie was soon leading the kind of life that's brought to you by the letter X—for x-rated, that is. By the time she arrived on *Capitol,* she'd already been involved with *Penthouse* publisher Bob Guccione and had turned Hugh Hefner down flat. For starters, Leslie had refused to pose for *Playboy* unless Hefner was willing to pay her $35,000. "Then maybe it would be worth it to be pinched on the ass by all your fat friends," she told him.

But Leslie's bravado was just a masquerade. Despite her tough and torrid veneer, she was really a

Spitfire Leslie Graves went into a tailspin after the death of her Capitol *mom, Carolyn Jones.*

rather fragile soul, desperately in need of a guiding hand. For a while she found it in veteran actress Carolyn Jones, who played her mother, Myrna Clegg, on *Capitol.* Carolyn had been through several stormy marriages—including one to *Dynasty* producer Aaron Spelling—and had no children of her own. She was famous for befriending the kids she worked with and showering them with motherly affection. (Over the years, she was paticularly devoted to young actress Lisa Loring, who'd played her daffy daughter, Wednesday, on the long-running TV series, *The Addams Family.*)

On *Capitol,* Carolyn quickly took Leslie Graves in tow—and became her star protector on and off the set. And when Carolyn announced she was getting married—yet again!—Leslie eagerly joined in the festive wedding preparations.

On September 26, 1983—six months after *Capitol* debuted—the whole cast gathered at a West Hollywood restaurant to witness Carolyn's marriage (her fourth) to actor Peter Bailey-Britton. Also on hand were long-

The late Carolyn Jones won an Oscar nomination for 1957's Bachelor Party. *Future* Knots Landing *star Don Murray was her leading man.*

time friends and costars Sally Struthers, Red Buttons, and John Astin (who'd played Carolyn's husband on *The Addams Family*).

But the bliss was short-lived. Just a few months later, Carolyn was stricken with double pneumonia, and paramedics had to be called to the house three times when breathing complications developed. She eventually recovered from the pneumonia, but tests revealed that she was suffering from an incurable form of cancer. She died before the end of 1983.

The entire cast was stunned, but Leslie Graves seemed to take it the hardest. After the death of her best pal and backstage mom, Leslie became increasingly lethargic and depressed on the set. She'd stay in her dressing room for long periods of time; more and more, she had trouble coping with the pace and pressure of the grueling daily schedule. Finally she took a leave of absence and began seeing a therapist. When she came back to the show, she seemed in good shape, but her heart was no longer in it. As soon as her contract was up, she left for good.

■   ■   ■

During her Hollywood heyday, *Falcon Crest*'s Kim Novak was one of the most volatile stars on the studio horizon. In the mid 1950s she was literally manufactured as a screen commodity by Harry Cohn, head of Columbia Pictures. At that time Kim was a total unknown, with almost no acting credentials, but Cohn was determined to create a new Columbia sex kitten to replace Rita Hayworth, who'd just walked out on him—and physically Kim more than fitted the bill.

But her voluptuousness didn't always fool the cameras. When Cohn forced director Josh Logan to give Kim the lead in *Picnic,* she found it impossible to cry on cue. Logan had to grab her by the shoulders and keep shaking her in order to get the tears to come. Getting her to exhibit any real emotion at all was even harder.

Nevertheless, Columbia kept pushing and publicizing Kim Novak, and in this case the hard sell worked. During the 1950s Kim became a box-office favorite and even appeared in a few memorable films (*Vertigo, Pal Joey, Bell, Book and Candle*), but her on-screen life was tame compared to her off-screen hijinks. Her most scandalous involvement was her so-called "friendship" with married playboy Rafael Trujillo, Jr., son of the dictator of the Dominican Republic. He lavished Kim with expensive jewels and sportscars, and at one point their dates even became a matter of national debate in Congress.

In his autobiography, *Yes I Can,* Sammy Davis, Jr., asserted that he was one of Kim's former flames. According to Davis, he rented a beach house at Malibu, specifically so they could meet in secret. In those days the slightest hint of an interracial romance could easily have jeopardized their careers.

In the early 1960s Kim married British actor Richard Johnson, but their marriage, like *Moll Flanders,* the film they made together, didn't enjoy a very long run. Within a year Kim was on her way to divorce court, and the breakup (combined with her deteriorating film career) sent her into an emotional tailspin. Kim cut herself off from everyone and was rumored to be on the verge of a breakdown. She went into intensive therapy, left Hollywood, and stopped acting for more than a decade. In 1980 she made her screen comeback, with Liz Taylor and Rock Hudson, in *The Mirror Crack'd.*

During her long hibernation from show business, Kim threw off her glossy manufactured image and finally got in touch with her real feelings. For the first time in her life, she was able to have a truly satisfactory relationship with a man—and her knight in shining armor, a veterinarian named Robert Malloy, helped Kim find the happiness that had always eluded her. In the mid-1970s she married him, and today they live in virtual isolation on their California ranch, raising horses and llamas.

■   ■   ■

On One Life to Live, *Judith Light had many a stormy encounter with Steve Fletcher, who later changed his name to Steve Blizzard.*

In a profession that's given us Barbra Streisand and BarBara Luna, there's frequently nothing ordinary—or real—about an actor's name.

It's easy to understand why *Falcon Crest*'s Marlene Wasden became Abby Dalton or why *As the World Turns'* Mary McClarty prefers to be called Eileen Fulton. But the short-lived celebrity of the one and only Steve Blizzard is quite another story.

Mr. Blizzard was a performer on *One Life to Live,* who originally went by the name of Steve Fletcher. After several years on the show, he fell in love with an actress named Nana Visitor (who'd once appeared on *Ryan's Hope*). Life was very uncomplicated until one winter's day in New York. Steve was horsing around in the snow with Nana's brother and during the roughhousing a bet was made: if Steve couldn't belly-slide a certain number of feet, he'd have to change his name to whatever new name Nana and her brother chose for him. Well, Steve lost the bet and—in honor of the snowfall that had precipitated the wager—Nana picked the name Blizzard.

Steve's checks, credit cards, driver's license—even his name on the *One Life to Live* video crawl—were all changed from Fletcher to Blizzard, and that's the way he was known for several years. But then Steve and Nana broke up—and he was so upset that he went right back to Fletcher. Well, if Farrah Fawcett could drop Majors, it's only fair, isn't it?

BACKSTAGE
AT
THE SOAPS

When it comes to soap opera storylines—the ones that make it to the screen and the ones that don't—there's a lot more involved in fashioning that final script than meets the eye. Actors can create all sorts of roadblocks when there's a storyline they don't want to play. For many years, Beverly Penberthy portrayed Pat Randolph, a leading heroine on *Another World*. Her character stood trial for murder, became an alcoholic, lost her husband to another woman—in other words, endured all the usual soap opera anguish—and Beverly never winced. But one storyline sent her storming into the producer's office in a roaring fit. When the script called for Pat Randolph to urge her unwed, college-age daughter to have an abortion, Beverly—a devout Roman Catholic—absolutely refused to play the scene. To pacify her, the script had to be rewritten so that Pat Randolph didn't find out about the abortion until after it took place.

That's an extreme example, perhaps, but head-on collisions between actors and writers aren't infrequent occurrences. Few stars are ever happy one hundred percent of the time. If they're working only two days a week—and busy collecting dust on the show's back burner—they groan about feeling creatively unfulfilled. If they're caught up in a major storyline—and working four or five days every week—they gripe about getting burned out and exhausted. It's a standing joke in the daytime television industry that actresses who don't work enough get headaches; actresses who work too much get migraines.

It's also a pretty worn-out record that actresses who play heroines secretly yearn to be homewreckers. That's why *Dynasty* came up with the idea of an evil look-alike for pure and saintly Krystle Carrington. If Linda Evans had to pour one more cup of tea—or dredge up one more ounce of sympathy—on-screen, she probably would have been ready for the booby hatch.

It's a definite fact of soap opera life: heroines may be beloved, but they're basically boring. And actresses who play them can't help climbing the walls after a while. Viewers literally worship Victoria Lord Buchanan, but *One Life to Live* periodically sends her into a schizophrenic funk just so her tacky alter ego, Nikki Smith, can emerge. It usually happens when Erika Slezak, who plays Vikki, is starting to develop cream-and-sugar elbow (from serving all that coffee), not to mention an allergic lint reaction (from fluffing all those pillows). Turning haughty Vicky into naughty Nikki gives Erika a chance to bust loose. As Nikki, she gets to have sordid love affairs, sit in sleazy bars, wear low-cut dresses, and tell all the town stiffs to shove it!

Not everybody wants to be queen of the slime pit, though. Despite the built-in yawn factor, some actresses would give their eye teeth to play a slightly nauseating goody two-shoes for a change. Why? For one thing, heroines generally have a longer lifespan on soaps—they don't get carted off to jail or murdered—or condemned to some murky storyline oblivion for their miserable misdeeds.

They don't get hate mail, either. Faithful daytime fixtures like Erika Slezak are treated like national treasures. Fans send them fruit cakes for Christmas and knit them sweaters on their birthdays. Meanwhile, actresses who play lowlifes and losers sometimes get threatening letters and need bodyguards—not to mention the verbal and physical abuse they receive from fans who can't distinguish between fantasy and reality. During Lisa's heyday as a harridan on *As the World Turns,* Eileen Fulton sometimes needed a police escort just to leave her West Side Manhattan apartment every morning. A particularly flaky fan once stopped her in the street and slapped her across the face. Another disgruntled viewer threatened to maul her with a grapefruit when he caught Eileen peacefully squeezing melons in her neighborhood supermarket. No wonder some actresses would rather play the victim than the vamp.

■　　■　　■

Even love scenes can be a real turn-off. Forget AIDS and herpes for a minute; catching pneumonia on-screen can be a danger, as well. As *General Hospital*'s Anna Devane, Finola Hughes was required to do some hot and heavy rolling in the sand with costar Tristan Rogers (Scorpio) and their

From Here to Eternity–style beach capers were taped on location in Santa Barbara. The scenery was picturesque, but the beach that day was actually freezing. "The ocean was so cold you could have chilled champagne in it," Finola remembers, "but when you're on location with a soap there

"The Chill of It All": That's what General Hospital's *cast nicknamed this teeth-chattering beach scene between Tristan Rogers and Finola Hughes.*

isn't the time or money to wait for the weather to warm up. So Tristan and I had to run around in that icy water pretending to be languorous with passion. Actually, our teeth were chattering and our knees were shaking. We're lucky we didn't get frostbite."

.　　.　　.

Emma Samms went to the opposite extreme on *General Hospital*. When she and Tony Geary taped a highly dramatic chase scene at L.A.'s Magic Mountain amusement park, the temperature rose to over a hundred degrees. After working in the scorching sun for several hours, Emma nearly passed out from heat exhaustion.

But even the weatherproof confines of the studio can't guarantee total protection from the elements. Bed scenes are particularly unpopular because most sets are drafty and give everybody a real case of "cold feet."

"All they let you wear under the covers is a very skimpy flesh-colored body stocking," says one actress. "You're nervous about doing the scene to begin with, so that makes you even colder. By the time your leading man has to touch you (he's just wearing shorts!), you're both so cold and shaky, it's like ice touching ice! But sometimes, when the director isn't looking, I'll put on legwarmers just before taping, and pray the covers don't fall off me when we're doing the scene!"

Occasionally a starlet who's a novice will try to bring a hot-water bottle on the set—and backstage legends abound about soap actors, past and present, who've kept flasks of whiskey hidden under the pillow so they could calm their frightened leading ladies, and warm them up a bit, just before taping a bed scene.

.　　.　　.

Rape scenes are even rougher to do—and some actresses have nightmares for weeks afterward, reliving the agony of their on-screen ordeal.

Probably the most famous rape in soap opera history was Luke Spencer's dance-floor assault of Laura Baldwin, which began as a brutal physical attack and then developed into a surprise love story. The day of the taping the *General Hospital* studio was closed to outsiders, and Genie Francis, who was only eighteen, stayed hidden in her dressing room until just moments before she was needed on set. She was literally shaking like a leaf. Luckily, she happened to have a very thoughtful and understanding costar. Tony Geary not only choreographed each move of the rape down to the finest detail (so he could be sure not to accidentally hurt her), he even sent her flowers that day to remind her that she could trust him.

"I was very worried about her," Tony explains. "Genie was so young and very inexperienced as an actress. I knew we had to pull out all the stops to make the scene good, but at the same time I didn't want to traumatize her. We had to tread a very careful line." According to observers on the set, Tony held Genie in his arms after the scene was shot and they both wept, because they were so emotionally drained from what they'd just been required to act out.

■   ■   ■

Other actresses have been plagued by recurring nightmares after doing a rape storyline or gone into a mild depression for a while. Nobody denies that rape stories are big ratings-boosters, but they definitely take a heavy toll on the performers involved.

Tina Johnson possibly had the hardest job of all. A few years back, when she was starring on the now defunct soap opera *Texas,* her character, Lurlene Harper, was scheduled to be sexually assaulted. "The writers didn't know it," says Tina, "but they were asking me to relive my own life story. Sometime before that I'd been attacked by a rapist. He beat me up very badly, but fortunately I fought him off and was able to get away. Still, it left me shaken for a long time. I didn't feel comfortable doing this storyline on *Texas* because of the memories it brought back, but I didn't want to do anything to upset the apple cart. I didn't feel right going to the producer and refusing to do the story—I felt I had a commitment to the show, an obligation as an actress to do my job. So I said to myself, 'Tina, stop being silly—you can do this!' But the day of the taping, it started to get to me. Finally, during rehearsal, I just broke down and cried and cried. I didn't think I could get through it. Fortunately, our director, Andy Weyman, was a very sensitive man. He sat and talked with me, and got me to see how I could use my fear and anger effectively in the scene, how I could get it to work for me, and I did. He really helped me through it."

■   ■   ■

Next to rape, illness is probably the most unpopular storyline. Why? "Because you have to go out of your way to look bad!" shrieks one ABC starlet who was hospitalized on her soap with a bizarre and debilitating illness for four months. "You can't wear makeup, you can't get your hair done—you start to look and feel like a walking zombie. It's so depressing sitting in your dressing room and watching other actresses walk by on their way to wardrobe. Then you see them coming back with all these gorgeous designer clothes slung over their shoulder—it makes you want to scream."

Aside from vanity, there's another reason why nobody wants to be a soap opera invalid. Hospital beds aren't very comfortable. "I was coming home from the studio sore and achy all over," remembers one actress, whose character hovered between life and death on the air for several weeks. "You have to do your scenes with tubes coming out of your mouth and bandages all over your face, and you can't move—you can't even scratch an itch! It's enough to make you break out in hives!"

Playing an alcoholic also makes some stars cringe. "All you get to wear is shapeless housedresses and they fix your face up to look like a corpse," one barstool veteran reveals. "After months of playing that kind of depression, I'd leave the studio feeling blue and moody. I really needed a drink when I got home."

■   ■   ■

Maternity doesn't make a big hit with some actresses either. "I begged them not to let my character have a baby, but the writers went and did it, anyway," says Elvera Roussel, who used to play Hope Spaulding on *Guiding Light*. "I knew that was the end for me as a romantic heroine."

Why is on-screen motherhood such a forbidding prospect? "For one thing it limits your storyline options," explains *All My Children*'s Julia Barr. "Since my character, Brooke, became a mother, it's hard for her to go off and have wild and reckless love affairs. Viewers want her to be serious and sensible now."

Other actresses complain about the wardrobe limitations. "Wearing padded clothes for all those months is a real drag." moans one brand-new on-screen mother. "Worse yet, I'm a very suggestible actress. If my character gets a cold, so do I. So for three months I had morning sickness on and off the set. But the look on my face was nothing compared to the way my boyfriend looked. When he thought I was pregnant, boy, did he turn green!"

■   ■   ■

Stephen Schnetzer—in his infamous Crystal Lake incarnation—got aching feet and a lot of dinner invitations from the crew.

But Stephen Schnetzer—better known as *Another World*'s Cass Winthrop—had an even tougher assignment. A few years back, in a kind of daytime takeoff of *Tootsie*, his character had to go incognito as a very tacky dame named Crystal Lake. To prepare for the role, Stephen consulted with Dustin Hoffman's stage dresser, Frank Piazza, who taught him how to walk and gesture in perfect feminine style, without mincing or swishing outrageously.

For his first appearance on camera, Stephen chose a high-fashion outfit and a glamorous wig with a Joan Collins coiffure. Then he spent two hours in the makeup room. "It got a little competitive in there," Stephen laughs. "The makeup people were spending so much time on me that some of the actresses were starting to get jealous. There was also a lot of kidding. By the end of the first day, every guy in the crew wanted to buy me dinner!"

Stephen's debut as Crystal Lake got rave reviews from everyone, including his wife, actress Nancy Snyder, but he was glad when the story-line ended and he went back to button-down shirts and three-piece suits. "The wig hurt my head and the high heels pinched," he grumbles. "I felt like a chiropractor's nightmare." But through it all, Stephen never entirely lost his sense of humor. When someone asked which bathroom he intended to use, he winked enticingly and whispered in his best Marilyn Monroe voice, "Maybe I'll try both."

S.O.B.
AWARDS

Oscars, Emmies, Grammies, Golden Globes—Hollywood, a town that thrives on separating the winners from the losers, delights in giving out awards.

But in spite of all the balloting and ballyhoo, critics' prizes and popularity contests, some contributions—especially in the field of soap opera—are never recognized. These achievements, both great and small, may not necessarily rate an Irving Thalberg or an Antoinette Perry citation, but they're all definitely deserving of Soap Opera Babylon awards—S.O.B.s for short.

And now the envelopes, please . . .

Most Creative Casting

To *The Colbys:* for casting sixty-three-year-old Charlton Heston as the husband of thirty-eight-year-old Stephanie Beacham and the lover of forty-one-year-old Katharine Ross. At the same time, Beacham, in reality, is only eleven years older than Tracy Scoggins, who plays her daughter, and Katharine Ross' TV son, John James, would be far more believable as her leading man. He's barely a decade younger than she is.

Most Regrettable Career Decision

To George Peppard: for winning the role of Blake Carrington, then walking off the set of the *Dynasty* pilot in a huff and handing the role over to second-choice John Forsythe.

The Colbys *cast (l-r): Ken Howard, Tracy Scoggins, Charlton Heston, Stephanie Beacham, and Barbara Stanwyck. In reality, Tracy and Stephanie are closer in age to sisters, rather than mother and daughter.*

The Promises Are Made to Be Broken Award

To Patrick Duffy: for leaving *Dallas* in May 1985 and vowing never to return.

The Fear of Success Award

To *All My Children*'s Susan Lucci: for not only losing the Emmy sweepstakes seven times, but for her unique knack of losing more than a dozen leading men in sixteen years.

The Soaps' Sensitivity Award

To the former producer of *The Guiding Light:* this man—obviously not a *Family Ties* or *Eight Is Enough* lover—was horrified to learn that a young married actress on his show had gone off and gotten pregnant—without consulting him. When she blissfully confided her good news, instead of congratulating her, he roared, "What's the matter, didn't you ever hear of the Pill?"

Creative Negotiating Award

To Eileen Fulton, Jacqueline Courtney, and Barbara Stanwyck for their unique achievements in the field of contract bargaining: during her days as *As The World Turns'* reigning prima donna, Ms. Fulton became the first actress to have a clause written into her contract preventing her character from becoming a grandmother. While playing Alice Frame, the most popular heroine in *Another World* history, Ms. Courtney demanded and got a dressing room with a private bathroom—the only one in the entire studio building. And during her year on *The Colbys,* Ms. Stanwyck's contract stipulated that she could never work more than two days a week, never work past 6 P.M., and never work the week before Christmas—so she could do her shopping.

The Unjust Deserts Award

To the Unknown Soap Opera Actor who toiled from 7 A.M. till 5 A.M. the next day—a total of twenty-two hours—taping a difficult location sequence in the pouring rain and who was then fired for missing work when he developed bronchial pneumonia.

The Actors Guild Job Security Awards

To *Dynasty:* for firing Pamela Sue Martin when she asked for a raise.
To *Dynasty:* for replacing Catherine Oxenberg when she asked for a raise.
To *Dynasty:* for writing off Geoffry Scott. He probably asked for a raise.
To *Dynasty:* for always giving Joan Collins a raise.

The Truth in Advertising Award

To Lorenzo Lamas: for being the prime-time superstud linked with the most women—in the most supermarket tabloids—in a single week.

The You Gotta Be Kidding Award

To Priscilla Presley for having to deny all of the following tabloid stories in a single week: (a) that she communicates with Elvis' ghost (b), that she dumped Burt Reynolds for Julio Iglesias' doctor (c), that her teenage daughter, Lisa Marie, had been kidnapped by space aliens and/or a California religious cult.

The Golden Turkey Award

To NBC's *Flamingo Road:* for failing dismally in the ratings despite the presence of a cast that included Mark Harmon, Morgan Fairchild, David Selby, John Beck, Kevin McCarthy, and Barbara Rush.

The That's What Friends Are for Award

To Jane Wyman: for not phoning old friend Mel Ferrer to break the news to him personally when his role on *Falcon Crest* was being terminated.

Most Imaginative Costuming Award

To *General Hospital:* for making actress Emily McLaughlin wear the same black sweater on the air for twenty-three years.

The Indian-Giver Award

To *Dallas:* for giving—and then taking back—Ray and Donna's hearing-impaired adopted child.

The Consistency in Broadcasting Award

To *Dallas:* for pretending that Bobby's death never happened—and leaving *Knots Landing* holding the bag. Pam may have only dreamed Bobby's death, but on *Knots Landing* his brother Gary shed real tears for him and, as a loving memorial gesture, Val even named her baby after him.

The Soap Hack-Writer Award

To every scriptwriter who reaches (out of desperation) for the following soap opera clichés: a mysterious look-alike, an evil (or demented) twin, a woman impregnated by her husband's brother, a man who miraculously returns from the dead, a dining-room tracheotomy, a snowstorm that forces a woman to give birth in a secluded country cabin, a forty-five-year-old heroine who suddenly discovers she's adopted, a fatal blood disease that goes into permanent remission, any form of amnesia, mothers who cheerfully stand trial for murders they didn't commit in order to shield an errant child, cops who fall in love with their female patrol partners, and couples who get divorced even though they passionately love each other.

The Gullible-Fan Award

Last but not least, to every soap opera fan who thinks that Miss Ellie can really cook, that Krystle never screams at her baby, and that the service is always excellent at Ruby's waterfront diner in Port Charles.

Someday you're in for a helluva surprise.